CBT for Personality Disorders

SAGE has been part of the global academic community since 1965, supporting high quality research and learning that transforms society and our understanding of individuals, groups and cultures. SAGE is the independent, innovative, natural home for authors, editors and societies who share our commitment and passion for the social sciences.

Find out more at: **www.sagepublications.com**

CBT for Personality Disorders

Henck van Bilsen and Brian Thomson

Los Angeles | London | New Delhi
Singapore | Washington DC

SAGE Publications Ltd
1 Oliver's Yard
55 City Road
London EC1Y 1SP

SAGE Publications Inc.
2455 Teller Road
Thousand Oaks, California 91320

SAGE Publications India Pvt Ltd
B 1/I 1 Mohan Cooperative Industrial Area
Mathura Road
New Delhi 110 044

SAGE Publications Asia-Pacific Pte Ltd
33 Pekin Street #02-01
Far East Square
Singapore 048763

Library of Congress Control Number: 2010932193

British Library Cataloguing in Publication data

A catalogue record for this book is available from
the British Library

ISBN 978-1-84920-293-0
ISBN 978-1-84920-294-7 (pbk)

Typeset by C&M Digitals (P) Ltd, Chennai, India
Printed by CPI Antony Rowe, Chippenham, Wiltshire
Printed on paper from sustainable resources

CONTENTS

ABOUT THE AUTHORS

Henck van Bilsen is a consultant CBT and consultant clinical psychologist. He specialises in complex and long-standing problems and regularly presents at national and international conferences. Henck celebrated his 25th anniversary as a clinical psychologist in 2004. He initially trained in the Netherlands before gaining accreditation with the British Association for Behavioural and Cognitive Psychotherapies (BABCP). He is also accredited as a trainer and supervisor by the BABCP. He has been on the board of professional organisations like the Behavioural and Cognitive Psychotherapies and the Division of Clinical Psychology. He currently divides his time between the CBT Partnership and Canterbury Christchurch University as Director of CBT Programmes. In collaboration with Brian Thomson, he was instrumental in setting up and running the postgraduate diploma in CBT at the University of Hertfordshire.

Henck previously he held positions as the academic director of the Auckland Institute for Cognitive Behaviour Therapy (New Zealand), consultant clinical psychologist (personality disorders) and deputy director of the Pedologisch Instituut Rotterdam (the Netherlands). Since 1990 he has worked in private practice.

Brian Thomson is a senior lecturer at the University of Hertfordshire where among other things he has responsibility for teaching on the MSc programme in CBT. Brian's background is in community mental health where he worked as a CPN for many years, specialising in the treatment of personality disorders. In 2003 Brian completed a systematic review of evidence for effective treatment of personality disorders and has contributed a chapter to a book on caring for people with personality disorders. Brian maintains a small caseload in private practice and works as a senior associate with Hertfordshire CBT Partnership where he leads the Huntingdon branch.

INTRODUCTION

A search of 'personality disorders' on the Amazon website comes up with almost 3000 book titles (July 2010). Clients who receive a diagnosis of personality disorder are seldom happy with such a verdict and clinicians upon being informed that their next client has a diagnosis of personality disorder are rarely looking forward to the encounter. Without any doubt, people with a diagnosis of personality disorder often make their own lives and those of people close to them very difficult. They also pose significant difficulties for clinicians trying to assist them. In this book, we want to focus on an idiosyncratic approach to clients with a diagnosis of personality disorder as opposed to a categorical approach. Our approach will be based on individualised analyses of the specific personal, interpersonal and societal problems of clients and not on a categorical approach, whereby a client is offered programmatic and protocolised interventions when they are deemed to fulfil the criteria of a specific diagnosis.

Our cause is to convince the reader to see through the DSM/ICD diagnoses and observe the development, maintenance and functionality of the client's problem presentation while using the underpinning theory and practice of cognitive behavioural therapy (CBT). To assist us in our cause we invite the reader to take a transdiagnostic perspective on the phenomenon of personality disorder (Chapter 1). We will also postulate that CBT for personality disorders is 'just CBT and nothing special', like driving a big car on a long, narrow and winding road is just driving, but it should be done very slowly and carefully. In working with personality disorder it is essential to ensure the basics of CBT are done right (Chapters 2, 3, 4 and 5). In Chapter 6 we present a range of core interventions in working with personality disorders. Clients with a diagnosis of personality disorder are often (based on their history) sceptical about what a psychological therapy can do for them and clinicians may need to pay specific attention to how they engage and motivate clients (Chapter 7 focuses on engagement strategies and motivational interviewing). In working with clients who have been diagnosed with a personality disorder, the therapists need to understand their work in the larger context of societal perspectives on deviance, the cost of personality disorders to society and the evidence for psychological interventions; in Chapter 8 we will reflect on these issues. Working as a psychological therapist with personality disorders opens up a whole range of pitfalls, some of which are reviewed in Chapter 9.

Rather than presenting completely new ideas, our aim is to use the evidence, where possible, to underpin individualised CBT for people with a diagnosis of personality disorders. The examples used in the book are amalgamated examples of clients we have worked with and the names have of course been changed, as have essential details.

1
PERSONALITY DISORDERS OR NOT

In this chapter you will:

- Get an introduction to the concept of personality disorders.
- Receive information about diagnostic criteria for personality disorders.
- Be introduced to a transdiagnostic perspective on personality disorders.
- Be asked to contemplate whether a dichotomous approach (classification ICD, DSM) is the preferred approach or whether a continuum (transdiagnostic perspective) is a more helpful perspective.

The International Classification of Mental and Behavioural Disorders (ICD–10) defines a personality disorder as: 'a severe disturbance in the characterological condition and behavioural tendencies of the individual, usually involving several areas of the personality, and nearly always associated with considerable personal and social disruption'. The fourth edition of the Diagnostic and Statistical Manual of Mental Disorders (DSM–IV) defines a personality disorder as: 'an enduring pattern of inner experience and behaviour that deviates markedly from the expectations of the individual's culture, is pervasive and inflexible, has an onset in adolescence or early adulthood, is stable over time and leads to distress or impairment'. There are nine categories of personality disorder in ICD–10, while the DSM system proposes three broad clusters of personality disorders. Studies indicate a prevalence of 10–13 per cent of the adult population in the community (APA, 2000).

What is a Personality Disorder?

This is where the debate begins. Dobbert (2007) states that those with personality disorders have traits that cause them to feel and behave in socially distressing ways, typically resulting in discord and instability in many aspects of their lives. Depending on the specific disorder, these personalities are generally described in negative terms such as hostile, detached, needy, antisocial or obsessive. The assumption here is that the problem feelings and behaviours are the result of an underlying issue (a disorder) and that the disorder 'explains' the problem feelings and behaviours.

While many other psychological disorders fluctuate in terms of symptom presence and intensity, as with normal personality, personality disorders typically remain relatively constant throughout life, although they do vary in severity from individual to individual (Dobbert 2007). This is again an interesting statement. It means that the disorder is still there but at times it will be less visible or obvious (but how do we know it is still there if we can't see it?).

According to the Diagnostic and Statistical Manual of Mental Disorders (DSM-IV-TR) (APA, 2000), personality disorders can be categorised into three main groupings or clusters: cluster A encompasses odd or eccentric behaviours; cluster B encompasses those with dramatic, emotional, or erratic behaviour; and finally cluster C, encompasses those with anxious, fearful behaviour.

Cluster A is described in DSM-IV-TR as encompassing the following types of personality disorder: schizoid, paranoid and schizotypal.

Individuals with *schizoid personality disorder* (SPD) are detached from interpersonal relationships and show a marked restriction in the range of emotions they express. Those with SPD may be perceived by others as sombre and aloof, and often are referred to as 'loners'. According to the DSM system, to qualify for a diagnosis the person should at least demonstrate four of the following symptoms:

- Wishes not to have or to enjoy close relationships, family included.
- Prefers solitary activities and life.
- Has little or no interest in sex with other people.
- Has little or no pleasure when doing activities.
- Few if any close friends, other than first-degree relatives.
- Is indifferent to criticism or praise.
- Displays flattened affect, emotional coldness, or detachment.

People with a *paranoid personality disorder* (PPD) are typically distrustful and suspicious of others. Although they are prone to unjustified angry or aggressive outbursts when they perceive others as disloyal or deceitful, those with PPD more often come across as emotionally 'cold' or excessively serious. According to the DSM system, to qualify for a diagnosis the person should at least demonstrate four of the following symptoms:

- Believes without reason that others are exploiting, harming, or trying to deceive her/him.
- Has unjustified doubts about friends'/associates' loyalty or trustworthiness.
- Believes without reason that if she/he confides in others this information will somehow be used against her/him.
- Finds hidden demeaning or threatening meanings in harmless remarks or events.
- Is unforgiving and bears grudges.
- Believes without reason that people are out to attack his/her character or reputation and is quick to react with anger.
- Believes without reason in the infidelity of their sexual partner.

People with *schizotypal personality disorder* have a need for isolation and display odd, outlandish, or paranoid beliefs. In social situations, they may behave inappropriately or not interact with others at all, or they may talk to themselves. According to the DSM system, to qualify for a diagnosis the person should at least demonstrate five of the following symptoms:

- Ideas of reference.
- Magical thinking or odd beliefs, not consistent with the culture's norms, and influences behaviour.
- Odd perceptual experiences.
- Odd thinking or speech.
- Suspiciousness or paranoid.
- Narrowed or inappropriate affect.
- Eccentric, odd, or peculiar behaviour/appearance.
- Few or no close friends or confidants, not including first-degree relatives.
- Excessive social anxiety.

Cluster B includes the following types of personality disorders: antisocial, borderline, narcissistic and histrionic personality disorder.

A person with an *antisocial personality disorder* has a lack of empathy for the suffering of others and does not appear to have a conscience, has difficulty controlling impulses and manipulative behaviours. According to the DSM system, to qualify for a diagnosis the person should display from the age of fifteen a disregard for and violation of the rights of others, those rights considered normal by the local culture, as indicated by at least three of the following:

A   Repeated acts that could lead to arrest.
B   Conning for pleasure or profit, repeated lying, or the use of aliases.
C   Failure to plan ahead or being impulsive.
D   Repeated assaults on others.
E   Reckless when it comes to their own or others' safety.
F   Poor work behaviour or failure to honour financial obligations.
G   Rationalising the pain they inflict on others.

Research has shown that individuals with antisocial personality disorder are also indifferent to the threat of physical pain and punishment in general, displaying no indications of fear when threatened (Millon et al., 1998; Hare, 1999).

Someone with a *borderline personality disorder* (BPD) will find it challenging to regulate emotions. This emotional instability results in dramatic and abrupt shifts in mood, impulsivity, poor self-image and tumultuous interpersonal relationships. They are highly sensitive to rejection, and the resulting fear of abandonment may result in frantic efforts to avoid being left, with as a consequence suicide threats and attempts to force others not to abandon them.

Those suffering from BPD are also prone to other impulsive behaviours, such as excessive spending, binge eating, risky sex, and drug and alcohol abuse. They often exhibit additional psychiatric problems, particularly bipolar disorder, depression, anxiety and other personality disorders. Symptoms typically begin in early adulthood and, once present, can interfere with relationships, work performance, long-term planning and the individual's sense of self-identity.

According to DSM-IV-TR, to be diagnosed with BPD a patient must have a pervasive pattern of instability of interpersonal relationships, self-image and affect, marked by impulsivity beginning by early adulthood, as indicated by five (or more) of the following criteria:

- Frantic efforts to avoid real or imagined abandonment.
- Pattern of unstable and intense interpersonal relationships.
- Identity disturbance: markedly and persistently unstable self-image.
- Impulsivity in at least two areas that are potentially self-damaging (e.g., spending, sex, substance abuse, reckless driving, binge eating).
- Recurrent suicidal behaviour, gestures, or threats, or self-mutilating behaviour.
- Affective instability due to a marked reactivity of mood (extreme changes in mood typically lasting a few hours and only rarely more than a few days).
- Chronic feelings of emptiness.
- Inappropriate, intense anger or difficulty in controlling anger.
- Transient, stress-related paranoid ideation or severe dissociative symptoms.

A person with a *narcissistic personality disorder* (NPD) will demonstrate in behaviour, attitudes and thoughts grandiosity, need for admiration and lack of empathy. They tend to be extremely self-absorbed, intolerant of others' perspectives, insensitive to others' needs and indifferent to the effect of their own egocentric behaviour.

According to DSM-IV-TR, a patient must exhibit five or more of the following traits in order to be diagnosed with NPD:

- Grandiose sense of self-importance.
- Preoccupation with fantasies of unlimited success, power, brilliance, beauty, or ideal love.
- Belief that he or she is 'special' and unique and can only be understood by, or should associate with, other special or high-status people (or institutions).
- Need for excessive admiration.
- Sense of entitlement.
- Takes advantage of others to achieve his or her own ends.
- Lack of empathy.
- Envious of others or believes that others are envious of him or her.
- Arrogant, haughty behaviours or attitudes.

Individuals with *histrionic personality disorder* exhibit a pervasive pattern of excessive emotionality and attempt to get attention in unusual ways, such as bizarre appearance or speech. With rapidly shifting, shallow emotions, histrionics can be extremely theatrical, and constantly need to be the centre of attention.

According to DSM-IV-TR, a patient must exhibit at least five of the following traits:

- Uncomfortable if not the centre of attention.
- Interaction with others in an inappropriately provocative or seductive manner.
- Shallow and rapid changing of emotion.
- Uses appearance to draw attention.
- Speech that lacks detail and is excessively impressionistic.
- Theatrical, self-dramatisation, or out of proportion expression of emotion.
- Easily influenced, suggestible.
- Perceives ordinary and social relationship as intimate.

Cluster C includes obsessive compulsive, avoidant and dependent personality disorder.

People suffering from *obsessive-compulsive personality disorder* are focused on order and perfection. As a consequence their lack of flexibility interferes with their ability to get things done, and to enjoy life in general. Little is accomplished because, whatever the task, for the obsessive-compulsive, it is never right or good enough. These individuals become mired in detail and are often unable to see the big picture; a literal example of not being able to see the forest for the trees. The standards set for themselves and others are impossibly high, and they are prone to damage personal relationships by being critical of those who don't live up to their standards. There are few moral grey areas for someone with this personality disorder: things are either right or wrong, with no room for compromise. (Dobbert, 2007).

According to DSM-IV-TR, a patient must exhibit at least four of the following traits:

- Marked preoccupation with details, lists, order, organisation, rules, or schedules.
- Marked perfectionism that interferes with the completion of the task.
- Excessive devotion to work.
- Excessive devotion and inflexibility when it comes to ethics, morals, or values.
- Finds it impossible to throw out worn-out, useless, or worthless objects, with no sentimental value.
- Insists others work or do task exactly as they would.
- Views money as something to be hoarded.
- Stubborn and rigid.

Those with *avoidant personality disorder* experience an intense level of social anxiety. They are often extremely self-conscious, and as a result they tend to avoid social situations and gravitate to jobs that involve little interpersonal contact. They often feel inadequate or inferior to others and are hypersensitive to rejection. Unlike individuals with schizoid personality disorder, they *do* crave social relationships but feel that social acceptance is unattainable (Dobbert, 2007).

Avoidant personality disorder is only diagnosed when the characteristic behaviours are pervasive and disabling. According to DSM-IV-TR, a patient must fit at least four of the following criteria in order to be diagnosed with an Avoidant Personality Disorder:

- Avoids activities involving interpersonal contact.
- Unwilling to get involved with people unless they are certain of being liked.
- Shows restraint in intimate relationships due to a fear of shame or ridicule.
- Marked preoccupation of being rejected or criticised by others.
- Inhibited in new social situations because of feelings of inadequacy.
- Views self as socially inept, personally unappealing, or inferior to others.
- Reluctant to take personal risks or engage in new activities, for a fear of being embarrassed.

A person with a *dependent personality disorder* (DPD) is characterised by neediness. They want to be taken care of, cling to those they depend on and often rely on others to make decisions for them. They have a strong fear of rejection and may become suicidal when faced with a disintegrating relationship. Those with DPD require excessive reassurance and advice, and are commonly over-sensitive to criticism or disapproval.

The diagnosis can only be made when the characteristic behaviours are pervasive and very disabling. According to DSM-IV-TR, a patient must fit at least five of the following criteria in order to be diagnosed with DPD:

- Difficulty making everyday decisions without an excessive amount of advice.
- Needs others to assume responsibility for most major areas of his or her life.
- Difficulty expressing disagreement with others.
- Difficulty initiating projects or doing things on his or her own.
- Goes to excessive lengths to obtain nurturance and support from others.
- Exaggerated fears of being unable to care for him or herself.
- Urgently seeks another relationship when a close relationship ends.
- Preoccupied with fears of being left to take care of him or herself.

The Party

You are invited to a party and by chance you arrive early and have a good opportunity to observe all the guests as they arrive. You soon realise that this is a very interesting party with a bunch of rather special people. Could you decide which personality disorder would apply?

First you meet *Beatrice*. You notice that she has been drinking before the party; she is unsteady on her feet and needs the support of a wall or door. She tells everyone with enthusiasm that she is a much better driver with a few drinks inside her and that sometimes she likes to drive back and close her eyes for brief periods while driving. When someone comments that this sounds dangerous, she unleashes a stream of verbal abuse on the poor man. This is followed by collapsing in a chair in tears. Later in the evening you notice Beatrice being the centre of attention of a small group and she describes that she is always on top of the world, nothing can bring her down.

At exactly 8.30 p.m. the doorbell rings and there is *Keith*, dressed immaculately, and is pleasant and polite to everyone. You notice how Keith holds his drink in a very special way and that he seems to take sips at regular intervals. Keith also mingles well with the other guests. You notice, however, that he rarely has a real conversation; he talks with people for exactly six minutes and then moves to the next person. He frequently checks his watch and leaves at 10.15 p.m. exactly.

Lisa makes a dramatic entrance. She storms to the middle of the big lounge and shouts at the top of her voice: 'The party can start, I am here'. She continues to dominate every group she joins with stories about herself, mainly how marvellous she is and how lucky we all should feel to be in her presence. People seem to be irritated by her and when someone questions one of her all too fantastic stories about herself she gets so angry that she throws the contents of a glass in the other person's face.

Daniel makes a quiet entrance and quietly stands at a certain spot, without moving too much. He does not initiate any conversation, but when spoken to answers questions, though he does not volunteer anything or ask questions. People speak to him briefly before moving on, which does not seem to bother him. He is in the last group to leave, when several people have voiced that it is very late and that this is the end of the party.

Bob arrives at the party and is immediately full of stories about plans he has, schemes he is developing, opportunities he is creating and invites others to join in these plans. When asked for evidence of the potential success of these plans Bob tells charming stories about how successful he has been in the past and offers to help the host with dishing out food and refreshing people's glasses. It is obvious that as soon as someone has uttered a potentially critical comment on Bob's plans that he moves to a new group. You also observe that Bob hides several bottles of wine in his coat with a clear intent to take them home.

Jennifer has spent a long time debating with herself whether she should go to the party. She arrives late and hesitates for a while at the entrance of the room. She does not make eye-contact with anyone and when people speak to her she looks frightened and surprised. She spends most of her time at the party with her back to the group studying the pictures on the wall and the books in the bookcases. She leaves early.

You realise you have ended up at an unusual party in which all these people could probably be diagnosed with a personality disorder.

According to the official classification systems of mental health problems (DSMIV: APA, 2000) there are ten clinically recognised personality disorders, each characterised by problem feelings and behaviours that can create a life of instability. Would we be able to diagnose our friends at the party with these guidelines? The answer would be a tentative yes, but whether we all would agree on who fits which personality disorder would be questionable.

The concept of personality disorder is a difficult one. For instance there are more than 100 possible variations to comply with a DSM IV diagnosis of borderline personality disorder. So we could have one client receiving a diagnosis of borderline personality disorder who demonstrates frantic efforts to avoid abandonment, has a pattern of unstable relationships, threatens suicide frequently, demonstrates instability of mood and reacts at times with intense anger. We may encounter another client with the same diagnosis who demonstrates chronic feelings of emptiness, paranoid ideation, intense anger, identity disturbance and impulsivity.

In other words, a heterogenic group of people is captured under the umbrella personality disorder. No wonder that there are strong moves to focus more on dimensional model of personality disorder as opposed to the current dichotomous model (Widiger 1992). The research agenda for the next generation of DSM (V) is therefore focused on the continuity of axis 1 and axis 2 problems and attempts at defining/fine tuning the term disordered personality by using the factors of the five-factor model: neuroticism, agreeableness, conscientiousness, extraversion and openness (Verheul, 2005). Parker and Hadzi-Pavlovic (2001) state it very clearly: 'Current definitions of the Personality Disorders commonly combine descriptors of personality style and disordered personality functioning.' Attempts to link the most prominent personality theories with the thinking on personality disorders have not moved beyond an initial stage (Duggan et al., 2003) whereby it is stated that 'measures of personality disorder and personality are related to one another in a predictable manner, certain personality dimensions have positive associations with personality disorder (neuroticism) while others (extraversion) have a negative association with personality disorder' (2001: 20).

Having a diagnostic category that is unclear, to say the least, makes controlled research on treatment effectiveness that is based on these diagnostic definitions not very trustworthy. We are in effect in the same stage of development regarding personality disorders now as we were half a century ago with respect to anxiety disorders (Wolpe, 1958, 1964; Wolpe and Lazarus, 1966): we know some things work sometimes, with some patients in certain circumstances but we are in no position to proclaim the existence of effective evidence-based interventions for patients – in real life settings – with a diagnosis of personality disorders.

A different approach

Harvey et al. (2004) list as important transdiagnostic processes responsible for human misery: attentional processes; memory processes; reasoning processes;

thought processes; and behavioural processes. They evaluate the traditional diagnostic approach in comparison to a transdiagnostic approach. In the former the diagnosis gets meticulously established based on sets of strict criteria (resulting in treatment options fitting with the diagnosis), while in the latter the processes are analysed in detail. This detailed analysis makes the application of individual- ised treatment options to counter the unhelpful process possible. Harvey et al. (2004) state that a transdiagnostic process is the preferred model. First of all, thinking in diagnostic categories leads easily to an 'us and them' thinking. Whereby 'us' equals the 'good' people and 'them' implies 'bad' or 'mentally ill'. We have unfortunately seen many examples of this during their years of clinical practice. Staff clearly perceive people with a diagnosis of personality disorder as 'them' (to be despised, mistreated and judged) and not 'us' (respectable upstanding people). It also leads to easy stigmatisation. Harvey et al. (2004) also make the case that a classification/diagnostic approach is an impossible task with at the moment 350+ disorders described in the DSM manual (no person is capable of having this amount of information in their working memory): an impossible task for diagnos- ticians! They further argue that in a diagnostic approach, valuable personal and idiosyncratic is in danger of getting lost. It furthermore becomes very difficult to deal with co-morbidity in a categorical model as we see in the case presentation example on the next pages. From our perspective, we favour a transdiagnostic and problem-based approach, here not the diagnostic category but the processes involved in problem presentation, and the identified problems are analysed in an idiosyncratic model and form the basis of formulation and treatment.

Transdiagnostic Processes

Attentional processes

In many problem areas we can observe that people give more attention to certain issues and less to other issues. The process is general; the content is problem specific (Harvey et al., 2004).

In people with a diagnosis of personality disorder we can observe for instance focused attention on:

- Real and perceived personal put-downs (narcissistic).
- Personal discomfort (borderline).
- Self-serving opportunities (anti-social).

Memory processes

What people store in their memory, what they spontaneously remember and what they can deliberately retrieve seems to be very much habitual and again can be observed as a process in a variety of problem categories, but with a content specificity:

- Moments of despair are remembered better than moments of happiness by a person with a borderline personality profile.
- An occurrence whereby others do not treat him/her with reverence is stored away very well by a person with a narcissistic personality profile.
- When asked to come up with problem-solving solutions, a person with an anti-social diagnosis will retrieve more examples from memory that are 'illegal'.
- Reasoning processes.

How people apply reason to their lives is also described as a transdiagnostic process.

One of the branches of the tree of CBT, rational emotive behaviour therapy (REF), has identified four primary reasoning processes that lead to human misery:

- Demanding thinking.
- Catastrophic thinking.
- Self-downing thinking.
- Low frustration thinking.

Applying unsound reasoning seems a transdiagnostic process, but the exact content of the unhelpful reasoning seems to be connected to the specific problem area of the person.

Thought processes

How we use our brains is also a transdiagnostic process. Some people have one thought in their mind and ruminate about that endlessly, while others go in a flighty manner from thought to thought, while others again do both depending on the content of the thoughts.

The person with a narcissistic personality style may repeat over and over in their mind the imagined sleights other people have inflicted upon him, resulting in increasing anger. Someone with a borderline personality style may go from impulsive thought to impulsive thought, not concentrating on any, leading to a very unsatisfactory day.

Behavioural processes

A well-established transdiagnostic phenomenon is that people use behaviour to eliminate negative feelings and these behaviours may become very habitual. This general process gets problem-specific meaning, for instance the phenomenon to aim for short-term relief with long-term negative consequences is seen in:

- People with a borderline personality style (self-harm).
- Narcissism (bragging about never accomplished feats).

EXAMPLE

The Case of Peter

Peter is a 35-year-old man who has spent seven years in prison and was detained under the Mental Health Act (section 37) under the formal diagnosis of psychopathic disorder. He stayed for three years in a medium secure forensic hospital specialising in the treatment of personality disorders. His 'index offence' was trying to commit suicide by putting a big pot filled with petrol on an electric hob, which failed because the electricity fused out before it exploded. Potentially many people could have been killed. Before the index offence he had frequently been in contact with the police, mainly as a result of dramatic ways of attempting to end his own life. Peter had been a drop-out from school and college, and had never held a job. His pre- and post-prison life was also filled with excessive drugs and alcohol use.

Diagnostic/assessment information

During assessment, Peter qualifies for a diagnosis of anti-social personality disorder and borderline personality disorder, according to the Personality Assessment Inventory (Morey, 1997). He has a co-morbid substance abuse disorder (according to DSM IV criteria) and post-traumatic stress disorder (PTSD), related to some incidents with the police where the armed offender squad was called in to deal with Peter (based on the Post-Traumatic Stress Diagnostic Scale (Foa and Rothbaum, 1998). He has an elevated score on the anxiety inventory (50 out of 63), but not on the depression inventory (Beck et al., 1961). Young's schema questionnaire (Oei and Baranoff, 2007) reveals maladaptive schemas with respect to entitlement (90 per cent), insufficient self-control (75 per cent) and unrelenting standards (60 per cent). So where does this leave us with Peter? Does he have a personality disorder? Does he have an anxiety disorder? According to the DSM classification system, he would be diagnosable with anti-social personality disorder, borderline personality disorder, post-traumatic stress disorder and substance abuse disorder. Is this a case of four for the price of one, or has giving clients diagnostic labels become meaningless in this case?

Transdiagnostic processes applied to Peter

How helpful is it to have a client with this multitude of diagnoses? Does the list of diagnoses tell us something about the hierarchy or connections of the issues? Not really. A more productive approach would be to review Peter from a transdiagnostic perspective. Here is an overview of how the transdiagnostic perspective applies to

(Continued)

13

(Continued)

some of Peter's issues. This leads to a much clearer perspective on potential treatment options.

Attentional processes

We observe then that his attention is habitually focused on negative feelings and occurrences where his personal needs are not met. His attention is also drawn to opportunities to get his needs met and he is very inattentive to other people's needs.

Memory processes

He is inclined to store these moments better in his memory and, when asked to recall days, he will voluntarily describe how he has experienced negative feelings and how his personal needs have not been met.

Reasoning processes

His thinking is very much biased against life being fair to him and he demands fairness. He personalises events (when things do not go the way he wants them to go, he perceives it as a deliberate attempt by life to cause problems for him), he catastrophises and translates his personal wishes into demands. He is inclined to label effort and difficulty as 'too much' (I can't stand it.).

Thought processes

He is inclined to ruminate about negative events that have happened.

Behavioural processes

The behaviour he engages in to make life acceptable for him is using drugs and alcohol, engaging in high-risk behaviours and behaviours that infringe upon other people's rights/boundaries. When he encounters difficulties he is inclined to give up.

Formulation incorporating transdiagnostic elements

Peter is very demanding towards his own performance and achievements in life. As a result of his lack of self-control he seldom achieves what he perceives as his full potential. This triggers the entitlement core belief and results in strong negative affect (anger, guilt). The physiological arousal that comes along with strong negative affect is perceived as intolerable and results in anxiety thus kick-starting a vicious circle. His insufficient self-control means that he has no skills to deal with this apart from chemical escape strategies (drink and drugs) or dramatic gestures (dramatic suicide attempts). He has an over-learned response pattern of 'acting out' when he experiences negative emotions (and most emotions

(Continued)

Contemplating Personality Disorders

In this chapter we have made a case *against* a classification paradigm regarding personality disorders in *favour* of dimensional approach influenced by recent advances in the thinking about transdiagnostic processes.

We do not suggest abandoning the term personality disorder completely. What we do suggest is to look upon personality disorder as a continuum. Some people will feature at one end of this continuum with no traits present that are generally included in a diagnosis of a personality disorder. On the other end of this continuum will be people whose rigidity in attentional focus, memory processing, behavioural reaction patterns, reasoning and thought processes would be clear indications of personality problems. A dichotomous perspective is seen by us as unhelpful as it leads to labelling, stigmatising and an unhelpful 'disorder treatment focus' as opposed to a more helpful problem-treatment focus. In the following text we will use the term 'people with personality difficulties' to avoid the dichotomy trap.

Understanding check

Things you should be able to do after reading this chapter:

1 List the advantages and disadvantages of a dichotomous and a continuum approach to thinking about personality disorders.
2 Review the various categories described in a dichotomous approach: identify which disorders belong to categories A, B and C.
3 Review the specific characteristics of the various personality disorders from a classification perspective. For instance, what is needed for a diagnosis of: borderline personality disorder, anti-social personality disorder, schizoid personality disorder, dependent personality disorder and obsessive-compulsive personality disorder?
4 List the main transdiagnostic processes that are relevant for thinking about personality problems.
5 Apply the transdiagnostic processes to one or more personality disorder classifications.

2

CBT IN THE FRONT-LINE

In this chapter you will learn about:

- The key features of CBT.
- The main elements of the theories underpinning CBT.
- The *cognitive* basis of CBT
- The *behavioural* basis of CBT.

Nothing is as practical as a good theory! Kurt Lewin (1935, 1936, 1948) had it so very right when he said this. As cognitive behaviour therapists we operate in the real world as 'scientist-practitioners'. We cannot be practitioners alone; we have to use science to make sense of the phenomena we encounter. Science will also help us when 'practice as usual' does not produce the expected results. As scientist-practitioners we have to be able to use theory to think ourselves out of a practice problem. In other words when we apply therapeutic interventions 'as recommended' and they do not work 'as predicted' we need to use our knowledge and understanding of theory to work our way out of this.

Readers who are sitting on the edge of their chairs, eagerly anticipating completely new insights and new theories on people with personality difficulties will be deeply disappointed. One of the pitfalls of a categorical approach to psychological problems is the assumption that new theories and new intervention strategies are needed for each specific disorder. We would like to postulate that personality difficulties are a human phenomenon and that theories that explain human behaviour can be applied to people with personality difficulties. Personality problems are characterised by behaviours, emotions and cognitions that have become problematic. Learning theory and cognitive theory, the underpinning theoretical frameworks of cognitive behaviour therapy, can be used to explain how problem behaviours, emotions and cognitive processes emerge and how they are maintained. These theories apply to people with personality difficulties just as they apply to other people. A theory is like a map and if you want to find your way with a map it is important to match where you are with the pages of your map book. If you want to find your way in Lisbon, it is a futile exercise to study a map of London. You will not find your way. Similarly if you have the correct map and the situation is very complicated, it pays to be very careful and study the map and one's surroundings carefully. People with personality difficulties are complicated situations for psychological therapists and therefore the available theories need to be applied with great care.

In this chapter we will highlight key features of cognitive behaviour therapy and outline briefly the core theoretical components underpinning CBT.

Key Elements of CBT

Few psychological therapy approaches have generated as much interest over the last decades as CBT. Based on the notion that learning and thinking play roles in how emotional and behavioural problems emerge and how they are maintained, this therapy aims to reduce distress by unlearning maladaptive habits, changing maladaptive beliefs and providing new information processing skills.

CBT can be seen as a huge tree with many 'branches' such as rational emotive behaviour therapy (Ellis, 1970), dialectical behaviour therapy, acceptance and commitment therapy (ACT), mindfulness-based CBT and compassionate-based CBT. Despite their commonalities these approaches differ with respect to the processes that underpin change and the procedures to bring about change. All of these approaches have the following principles in common:

- Based on a cognitive and/or behavioural model of emotional disorders.
- Brief and time limited.
- Structured and directive.
- Problem orientated.
- Based on an educational model.
- Based on a collaborative therapeutic relationship.
- Using homework is an essential feature.
- Using a holistic conceptualisation of the client and the client's problems.
- Using problem-solving techniques.

All cognitive behavioural interventions attempt to influence change by influencing thinking (Mahoney, 1977). Even primarily in behavioural techniques (exposure) the change in thinking facilitates effective processing. Cognitive behavioural approaches focus on the way in which an individual interprets an event. Thinking plays a role in determining subsequent affect and behaviour. Thinking itself is influenced by existing moods and the consequences of prior actions (Bandura, 1986). Thinking plays a strong facilitative role in how emotional and behavioural disorders start and are maintained. Therefore, changing thinking can serve to bring about therapeutic change.

If we apply this to personality disorders and for the moment use the 'traditional' manner of describing them, then we can see that those diagnosed with:

- anti-social personality disorder often think in opportunities to get their own needs met and think less or not at all about the negative consequences for others;
- narcissistic personality disorder will often think about their brilliance and excellence and not about their personal flaws – if flaws are pointed out to them then the person pointing them out is responsible for the resulting negative consequences;
- borderline personality disorder often demonstrate an intolerance towards negative feelings ('I don't like this feeling therefore I should not feel like this!').

Within the framework of cognitive behavioural approaches there is some variation with respect to both processes and procedure. Some approaches focus on the modification of behaviours through skills training (Linehan, 1993) while others focus on changing of distortions of existing beliefs. Others seek to compensate for perceived deficits in cognitive skills (Kendall and Brasswell, 1985). The approaches also differ to the extent with which they incorporate imagery strategies, behavioural components and the variation of cognitive interventions.

Interventions are all based on a cognitive and/or behavioural model of human misery

An essential component of CBT is to understand as a therapist and help the client understand that there is a link between one's misery on the one hand and one's beliefs and behaviours on the other hand. The behavioural element means that in CBT there is an acceptance that problem behaviours and emotions have been learned. This learning process can be understood by applying learning principles of operant and respondent conditioning to human behaviour (Domjan, 2006).

EXAMPLE

Geoffrey was detained in a high-security forensic psychiatric institution where he had been staying for several years. He had killed both his parents in a moment of 'irritation'. He was the only child of parents who absolutely doted on him. They were financially very well off and nothing was too much for Geoffrey.

From a young aged he learned:

- Everything I do is perfect (his parents idolised him and admired everything he did, mistakes were never his fault).
- I can't make mistakes, I am brilliant (when things did turn out badly, the parents blamed others and with their financial power were able to smooth the way when Geoffrey did some really bad things as a teenager).
- I am entitled to get what I want (the parents gave in to every whim).

(Continued)

Geoffrey was 31 years old when met by the therapist and he had been incarcerated for four years. He had never left home, apart from going on lengthy business trips (as he called his absences from the parental home). In fact they were lengthy luxurious holidays whereby Geoffrey spent his time drinking alcohol and drug taking to excess. Each time when he returned home completely broke he had a new plan for a new business that just required a bit of money from mum and dad and he would really make it this time. The amounts of money he asked for had steadily risen and the last time he had demanded a huge sum of money (apparently the parents had agreed to give Geoffrey the money but with stringent spending controls). When confronted with the message that he would not be able to spend the money as and when he wanted, Geoffrey decided (his words) that his parents had to die so he could gain unlimited access to the money.

Geoffrey's act of killing his parents was the end-product of a life-long learning process, whereby he had learned that if he acted up enough, he would get what he wanted.

Interventions are brief and time limited

CBT therapists work in a focused way and they aim for time limited and brief therapies. This means that therapies are not offered on a completely open ended basis. All therapies are guided by identified problems and specific goals. This does *not* mean that therapy can only last a limited number of sessions; it means that therapist and client regularly evaluate progress and make a plan for the next period of sessions.

EXAMPLE

Geoffrey was seen by a cognitive behaviour therapist for five years. The reader may wonder how this fits with 'brief and time limited'. The way it fits is that during these five years there were 14 periods of therapy. Each period started with an identified problem and a goal that Geoffrey wanted to aim for. For instance, one of Geoffrey's first problems was 'No one understands me'. The goal identified for this problem was 'Expressing my opinions and thoughts to others'. The work done on this problem and goal was a series of communication skills training sessions (eight in total). At the end Geoffrey was very well able to listen to others, express his opinions and express feelings, but he decided not to use these skills as 'People should just know what I want, why should I have to go through the effort?'

A sound collaborative therapeutic relationship is essential

The therapist is very empathic and rewarding when the client contributes to the therapy. The therapist is also focused on getting the client's input to the agenda; even when the client presents issues for the agenda in a 'hidden' manner, the therapist puts them to the foreground and on the agenda. In the following case vignette (the first session with Rachel who was diagnosed as an avoidant personality disorder) the client is clearly reluctant to discuss her difficulties. By using empathic listening the therapist gradually gets the client to talk about her difficulties.

Therapist: Well, thank you, Rachel for coming back today. Our last session was a week ago and in that session, if I can just briefly summarise, you decided that you might want to give cognitive behavioural therapy a go to see if that might be helpful for you to overcome some of the obstacles that you have in feeling happy within yourself. Is that still the case?

Therapist comments: opening statement, checking if client still wants to go ahead with CBT.

Rachel: I don't know, as it's going to take a lot of time. Isn't it?

T: So you are wondering if it is going to take a lot of time? Well that might be an issue that we might want to talk a bit about today. One of the ways that we try to work when we do CBT is that at the beginning of each meeting we make what we call an agenda, which is a list of things to talk about to make sure that all the things that you are worried and concerned about get discussed and all the issues that I would like to discuss. So this sounds like one of the things that we might want to put on the agenda. Is that OK?

Therapist comments: linking client's question with agenda setting.

Rachel: Yes. OK.

T: So you said, 'Is it going to take a lot of time?' Are there any other things that you would like to put on the agenda?

Therapist comments: agenda setting.

Rachel: Well, it does seem very odd, doesn't it, coming to talk to a stranger about things, you know? It's not exactly getting on with it, is it?

T: So, it is odd talking to a stranger.

Therapist comments: reflection.

Rachel: Well, you just have to, you know, get your head down, stiff upper lip and I suppose that is what people will say – 'Just deal with it'. That is what life is like isn't it?

(Continued)

T: 'Stiff upper lip. That is what life is like.' So we have got three things so far that we might want to put on the agenda:

1. Is it going to take up a lot of time?
2. It is odd talking to a stranger about these things.
3. Would it not be better to have a stiff upper lip and to get on with life and ignore the fact that you are unhappy?

Any other things?

Therapist comments: sticking to agenda setting.

Rachel: I don't know. I don't know what I'm supposed to do here, do I? It isn't something I've done before, so I don't know how I'm supposed to behave.

T: I think you are doing quite well and you are talking about the things that seem to be of a concern to you and we are listing them as issues that we can talk about. That is also a very good point. 'How to do therapy.'

Therapist comments: rewarding client's input whilst continuing with agenda.

Rachel: I've just thought about six sessions of lessons on 'How to do therapy!'

T: So if we look at these four things:

1. Is it going to take up a lot of time?
2. It is odd talking to a stranger about these things.
3. Would it not be better to have a stiff upper lip and to get on with life and ignore the fact that you are unhappy?
4. How to do therapy. How does it work, this cognitive behavioural therapy?

Good points for the agenda. Anything else you would like to talk about today?

Therapist comments: reflection and structuring the session.

Rachel: You said that you would be putting things on the agenda.

T: That is very good. Thank you very much for reminding me of that. What I would like to talk about, is to make a list of problems you would like to resolve with therapy and what your goals would be to resolve these problems.

Therapist comments: rewarding client's input.

Rachel: I don't know if I don't know how it works. I don't know what to expect from it do I?

(Continued)

(Continued)

T: That is a good point.

Rachel: It's not as if you are going to come and help me with my work and help me get on with things in the house; is it? It's still me that is going to go back home and do everything that I have to do, so I don't know how I can make a list.

T: I think we just did. You said that what sounds like a real problem for you is the overwhelming amount of tasks that rest on your shoulders. Would that be correct? Is that a problem for you?

Therapist comments: reflective listening and translating the client's complaint into a therapy problem.

Rachel: It's just what has to be done and I don't see by talking to somebody how they can take that away. It's not going to change the fact that those jobs are there.

T: I'm not saying that it will change the amount of jobs. I am just enquiring whether where you are sitting is the enormous amount of tasks that you have to do, whether feeling overwhelmed by that, is a problem for you or whether you are happy with this level of being overwhelmed?

Motivational interviewing intervention (Overshooting): 'Are you happy ...?', hoping that the client will make a problem statement.

Rachel: It's not a question of being happy or not is it? It is just a question of it has to be done and if I can't cope with it, then that's my problem, isn't it?

T: Then if you are saying that you can't cope with it, it is indeed your problem. So shall we put that on the problem list? Not coping with the amount of tasks that you have to do?

Therapist comments: recognising a brick wall for now, so we put it on the problem list.

Rachel: I didn't say that I wasn't coping, did I? I am getting them done. I am getting everything done. If you put me down as not coping then it means I'm a failure doesn't it?

T: So if you do not cope with something that means in your own terms that you are a failure?

Reflection.

Rachel: Of course it does. What else does it mean? If you don't get things done then you have failed, haven't you?

Uncovering irrational rules for living and underlying beliefs.

(Continued)

T: Let us write down a few things, Rachel. One second…

Therapy time out.

Rachel: I'm not sure about this, you know. I feel worse now than when I came in.

T: So what you are saying is that by talking about these issues, it makes you feel worse?

Rachel: Being called a failure makes me feel worse. Being told I can't cope with things makes me feel worse.

T: So what exactly did I say that implied that I thought you were a failure?

Therapist comments: bringing the client's distortions to the foreground.

Rachel: I don't know. I don't remember. You said something about if I can't cope with things then I am overwhelmed. I don't remember.

T: Yes. I kind of reflected on what you said yourself about the enormous amount of tasks that you seem to have to do when you are at home and I reflected that you said that about these tasks; that you felt overwhelmed by them.

Rachel: I don't want to let anybody down.

Therapist comments: more of the client's irrational beliefs uncovered.

T: So can I write that down as a topic that I would like to discuss with you? That you do not want to let anybody down? So that really sounds like if you let someone down that would be terrible for you? Can I go back and deviate a bit from the agenda? You asked me was there something that the therapist, me, would like to put on the agenda and I said, 'Yes, I would like to talk about problems and goals for therapy', and we started to talk about that already. This is something I would also like to do in this session and that is also one of your points. I would explain how this therapy works and that coincides with one of your points and that overlaps quite nicely. Towards the end of the session I would like to hear from you what you thought of this session, what the good points were and where I could improve the way I do therapy that could help you.

Therapist comments: adding to the agenda and structuring the session.

Rachel: You want my advice?

T: Yes.

Rachel: I don't know anything about therapy, so I don't know.

(Continued)

T: Well, towards the end I will ask you what you thought about the session. You will probably realise that you know a lot more about therapy by then. So we have the following things on the agenda:

1. Is it going to take up a lot of time?
2. It is odd talking to a stranger about these things.
3. Would it not be better to have a stiff upper lip and to get on with life and ignore the fact that you are unhappy?
4. How to do therapy. How does this CBT work?
5. Looking at problems and goals.

In the last one we have already identified three things; the amount of tasks that you have to do that sometimes feel overwhelming, but if it feels overwhelming you immediately get a sense that you are a failure and that is very upsetting for you. It also means that you might let people down, which is also very upsetting for you. So we have already got a little bit of a problem to identify. I would like to explain what this type of therapy is, which is already on the list and I would like your feedback on the session and that is what is on the whole agenda. Anything to add to that?

Therapist comments: structuring the session, ensuring the client and therapist know what is going to happen.

Rachel: It seems like quite a lot.

T: Let's see how we get on. We have another 50 minutes left, so we have got a bit of time to explore some of these things. Where shall we start? Let me show you what I have written down.

Interventions are structured and directive

As can be seen from the case vignette, sessions start with the setting of an agenda and then follow the agenda. Setting the agenda is not always a straight-forward process, but a very important one. It allows for the therapist to be directive and allows for input from the client.

In the above transcript of the beginning of a first session the therapist demonstrates that, with a sceptical client like Rachel, it is important *and productive* to keep firmly on track, while safeguarding not to alienate the client.

Therapy sessions are problem orientated

The therapist focuses the therapy on the problems the client wants to resolve. Complaints are translated into workable elements that can be changed in therapy. Identifying clear and specific problems and goals at the beginning of therapy is very important in CBT. The next case vignette occurred towards the end of the first session where the therapist tried to establish some problems and goals for therapy.

T: Perhaps we could move on to the next point on the agenda, which was looking at problems and we identified some goals for therapy of things that you would like to achieve. There are a couple of things that I wrote down, but I am not quite sure whether I wrote them down correctly. So problems that are going on in your life at the moment that you are unhappy about: the way you deal with these issues and that we would identify as problems and what we identified so far in our first discussion. If you can remember, there were an enormous amount of tasks and at times you feel totally overwhelmed by the amount of tasks and feel you are not coping with these and then you think I am a failure and being a failure is something that is terrible. The other problem that you identified was that you are very much worried about what people think of you and if you have an idea that other people might have critical thoughts about you then you do your utmost to avoid that and you get very worried and anxious about that. The third problem that you identified was that you are very concerned about letting other people down; if that would happen it would make you very anxious and upset. Let us look at the first one. The sense that there is an enormous amount of work that you have to do and you feel overwhelmed by that. Is that a problem or did I misunderstand that?

Therapist comments: structuring the session by providing a summary and checking out his understanding of the issues.

Rachel: Yes. Because I feel like I am always snapping at people and I am short tempered, because I cannot get everything done. Even if I do manage to get everything in order then everybody comes home and the whole place is a mess again.

T: When your family arrives home and makes a mess how do you react to that?

Rachel: I get cross and I shout and I feel like I am constantly nagging people to put things away and I feel like they do not understand and do not appreciate how long it takes. You know I used to be a fun person. I just feel I am giving 500 per cent the whole time, but I look at myself and think why would anyone want to spend their life with me.

(Continued)

(Continued)

T: So you are saying that you used to be more of a fun person than you are now, you are giving 500 per cent of yourself, but you are still wondering whether someone would want to be with you. The way that it sounds is that you are working very hard to do a lot of household tasks to keep things in order. At the same time always this hard work does not result in you being pleased with yourself and being proud of yourself. All the hard work seems to go into a bottomless pit and it does not lead to you feeling ok and you are not proud of yourself.

Therapist comments: structuring the session, using summaries to help the client to explore the issues in more depth.

Rachel: It is like a black hole, which disappears as soon as everybody comes into the house. I have a friend, she is an elderly lady, and she always says no matter how much she did during the day, and she always reminds me that they did not have washing machines and things like that in those days, she always used to do her hair, put her lipstick on and take her pinny off before her husband came home. I do not have time, I mean I do not have a pinny you know, but …

T: So I also sense from the way you talk that you do not have time to look after yourself, to do things that are good for you. So how does that make you feel that you do not have time to do things for yourself?

Rachel: I feel like part of the furniture. I feel like I am just there when everyone gets home, just like the sofa and curtains and bizarrely I feel very grey and colourless.

T: Is that a good feeling? Is that the way you want to feel?

Rachel: No, it is not the way I want to feel. I feel like an overcast day. I do not feel that the sun is ever going to break through again.

T: So I will see if I can try to make sense of the issues that you have put forward. It sounds like the problem is the enormous amount of tasks that you have to do and the self-criticism that erupts when you do not complete these tasks. Would that be correct? The other problem we have is the enormous amount of tasks that you have to do and the kind of criticism that you expect other people might give you if you do not complete these. You worry a lot about that. The third problem identified is that you do not take time to look after yourself and to do things that are good for Rachel, which makes you feel part of the furniture, which is not how you would like to feel. Another

(Continued)

(Continued)

problem that you mentioned is all the good work that you do in the house then you sense that this is not appreciated by your family.

Therapist comments: structuring the session and remaining focused on establishing problems to work on.

Rachel: I feel really disloyal now saying that about them.

T: Well, in a previous session you said 'others do not appreciate how much energy it takes'. How does it make you feel that the family does not seem to appreciate your efforts and the 500 per cent energy that you put into looking after them. How does it make you feel?

Rachel: I should not have said anything.

T: Well if you put that aside for a second. How does it make you feel that the family do not appreciate how much the energy that you invest in the household?

Therapist comments: structuring the session, by being kindly assertive and pushing her 'counter therapeutic comments' aside.

Rachel: Like nothing really.

T: It makes you think that you are nothing and how does that make you feel that you think I am nothing.

Rachel: No, I do not think I am nothing, that is how I feel.

T: That is how you feel. Is that a good feeling?

Rachel: It is not a good feeling

T: It is not a good feeling. So it sounds like that there are a lot of things going on in your life that lead to not good feelings. I will see if I can draw this. If we have as an end result here 'not a good feeling'. The way you sit and the way you talk about it sounds like 'not a good feeling' is to do with you feeling anxious, worried and depressed or would there be any other feelings?

Problems need to be established by getting clients to explore how certain things make them feel. Issues that cause negative and unwanted feelings result in a stronger motivation to work on them than issues for which this is not the case. In CBT the therapist needs to identify issues that are connected with strong negative affect and these need to be linked with the possibility of change.

Sessions are based on an educational model

The aim of the cognitive behaviour therapist is to educate the client so that she or he becomes knowledgeable about CBT and can make sense of her or his problems from a CBT perspective. In the following case vignette the therapist explains the basics of CBT and checks with the client whether he has understood it.

H: We agreed that today I would spend some time talking about cognitive behavioural therapy and we would discuss if it would be of any benefit to you. Is that still OK?

Geoffrey: Yes, that is fine; I have of course read a lot about cognitive therapy so there may not be that much new you can tell me.

Therapist comments: client demonstrates his superiority. When this happens it is important not to react defensively.

H: Excellent, so you may have a head start. Well, CBT is based on the idea that the situation we find ourselves in at the moment is strongly influenced by our learning history. Our life's experiences have resulted in us learning lessons from life. What would be lessons that you have learned from life?

Geoffrey: Well, I learned to walk, to talk, to read and write.

H: Very good – any other lessons you learned from life?

Geoffrey: An important lesson for me was that you can't really trust people – they say they want to help you but then they let you down. I learned how important it was to take precautions against that.

H: Sounds like a valuable lesson you learned – what were the precautions you learned to take?

Therapist comments: the therapist takes an approach to teaching about the CBT model by asking the client questions and guiding him through the process instead of 'lecturing at client'.

Geoffrey: Never to take no for an answer and to make sure my needs are met, but society does not accept that.

H: That sounds like an important insight. You learned to make sure that your needs are met, not to take no for an answer. However, this lesson of life has a downside and that is that society does not approve, hence your presence in this esteemed institution.

Geoffrey: That's it in a nutshell!

H: That is exactly what lessons in life can do: we learn them, they serve us well for a period, but if we persist in following them then the negative consequences can start to outweigh the benefits. But because we have learned no other lessons from life we persist in living life based on this lesson. When this results in unpleasant consequences, we may find it difficult to change. Working to getting what you want is a good thing, but if you follow that lesson like you followed it … how would you evaluate the results?

(Continued)

Geoffrey:	It sucks, man – would you want to live here with all these psychos?
H:	So one foundation block of CBT is that we are the end product of a long learning process. The other foundation is that 'thinking makes it so', in other words, what we say to ourselves is hugely influential in how we feel and what we do.
Geoffrey:	Well, I certainly don't talk to myself, if that is what you mean. I am not crazy.
H:	What I mean is we are all constantly thinking and what we are thinking influences how we feel and what we do. People can be in the same situation but feel and act very differently. Can you think of an example where this happened?

The style is educational, but not in the format of lengthy lectures. The client is invited to think with the therapist and to learn from the dialogue.

Homework is an essential feature of therapy

In CBT the therapy sessions are important, but equally so are the 'learning' tasks the therapist and client negotiate for the client to undertake between the therapy sessions; these can take different forms, but are often agreed as 'behavioural experiments', intended to give the client the opportunity to try out and practise different or 'new' behaviour. A CBT session is usually only one hour every week or fortnight. Therefore, for the therapy to have an impact, the client needs to work on therapeutic tasks between the sessions.

Therapy proceeds according to the therapist's holistic conceptualisation

The therapy itself and the in-between session tasks are structured upon the therapist's understanding of the client's problems. For clients with mild to moderate problems who present for the first time to a therapist, this understanding may be based on a brief assessment of the issues upon which the therapist decides to offer the client a structured (protocolised) CBT intervention. For clients who have received CBT or other treatments before without success and for clients with severe problems, the therapist will opt for an in-depth and detailed assessment before deciding on an individualised treatment plan. A conceptualisation attempts to identify learning processes from the client's past and current maintenance factors.

The therapy uses problem-solving techniques

CBT breaks down problems into manageable units, identifying the roadblocks that hinder problem-solving abilities. It does not perceive human change as an all or nothing phenomenon. The beginning of a change process involves careful identification of problems and goals. These are often broken down into smaller segments, thus making them much more achievable. Subsequently, these are addressed with a range of therapeutic interventions and thus break down the 'problem wall' brick by brick and thereby assist the client to an optimal recovery step by step.

Why CBT?

The research evidence for the effectiveness of CBT is abundant. From Roth and Fonagy (2004) to the Guidelines from the National Institute for Health and Clinical Excellence (2005), CBT is considered the treatment of choice for many mental health problems (Beck, 1976; Beck et al., 1990). The scientific evidence is very robust and strong for a range of mental health problems e.g. depression and the anxiety disorders (with a few exceptions such as body dysmorphic disorder and hoarding). With schizophrenia there is evidence that CBT and family based CBT are effective in assisting clients to optimal recovery (Kingdon and Turkington, 1991), whilst for personality disorders there is indicative evidence (Linehan 1993; Giesen-Bloo et al., 2006), but by no means is it as robust as for depression, anxiety and schizophrenia.

Another consideration is that the bulk of evidence relates to standard CBT interventions such as behavioural activation, cognitive restructuring, exposure, response prevention and other standard techniques in CBT. The evidence gets somewhat thinner for more recent additions to the range of CBT interventions.

Theoretical Foundations

There are two theoretical elements to the cognitive behavioural understanding of human misery: cognitive and learning theory. If we accept that human misery consists of experiencing unhealthy negative feelings or behaving in an unhelpful way (drinking too much, violence and avoidance), then we need to understand how both cognitive and learning theory contribute to the development of these factors.

Learning theory

Learning theory encompasses a number of principles that explain how humans learn. The three most important of these are operant learning, respondent learning and modelling.

Operant learning

Many scientists and psychologists have studied this type of learning or 'conditioning', particularly in animals. One of the most well known is arguably

B.F. Skinner and his experiments with rats in the 'Skinner box'. This learning principle tells us that we learn as a result of the consequences of our actions. When we do things, our actions will produce a result. This could be an external event, e.g. saying 'Good morning' with a smile to our neighbour results in a reply of 'Good morning' from the neighbour. It can also be an internal event, e.g. when we see a dog and become anxious, we can reduce or eliminate the anxiety by crossing the street and putting distance between the dog and ourselves. Behaviours that are followed by positive or enjoyable consequences are inclined to happen more often, whilst behaviours followed by unpleasant consequences tend to be suppressed.

Sounds simple and easy, doesn't it? In reality it is far more complicated. For instance, the absence of something unpleasant happening seems to work as a reinforcer. This is in fact how many anxiety problems are maintained. If we take as an example the fear of abandonment (a predominant feature of many clients diagnosed with a borderline personality disorder), the fear triggers frantic attempts to, the fear prevent the abandonment happening. As a result of this, the person will never really experience that being abandoned is unpleasant, but not the end of the world. All the actions (clinging behaviour, demanding behaviour, self-harm behaviour) to prevent abandonment result mostly in not being abandoned and as a consequence *a predicted feared outcome* did not happen. We call this negative reinforcement: something unpleasant is taken away or is prevented from occurring.

In this form of learning there are four alternatives: two result in an increase in the frequency of the behaviour, while two others have a more reducing impact on behaviours.

Positive reinforcement occurs when behaviour is followed by a positive event, in other words the behaviour of the person 'operates on the environment' in such a way that something positive is produced. Let's take the example of Dad taking his little boy Johnny shopping on Saturday. As soon as Dad's shopping cart is half filled, Johnny starts to demand an ice cream in a loud and piercing voice that turns into a shriek when Dad postpones getting an ice cream. As soon as the ice cream is in Johnny's hand, he smiles and says: 'Thank you, Daddy'. The giving of the ice cream is called positive reinforcement. Johny's actions have produced this positive product from the environment.

Negative reinforcement occurs when behaviour is followed by the taking away of a negative/feared event. If we study the example of Johnny and his father we see that Johnny is a born behaviourist: by stopping his shrieking and crying upon receiving the ice cream he applies negative reinforcement to Dad's ice-cream-giving behaviour. And remember, reinforcement always leads to an increase in the frequency of the behaviour reinforced.

A word of warning: reinforcement is what happens, not what we say that happens. Giving an ice cream and saying that this is the last time is by no means as powerful as the act of giving the ice cream. Deeds speak much stronger than words!

Reinforcements can be very specific and are sometimes too specific for our own good. The father may believe he is reinforcing Johnny's good behaviour if he gives him the ice cream with a warning to behave nicely, but what is rewarded is the behaviour preceding the reinforcement. Punishments can be behaviour specific as well, but in a negative sense. They tell us what *not* to do; they do not tell us what to do instead.

Positive punishment occurs when the behaviour is followed by a negative event: a smack, a reprimand or criticism. This results in the suppression of the behaviour involved, in the presence of the punisher (one reason why classrooms turn into chaos when the teacher leaves the room!).

Negative punishment is comparable to negative reinforcement: something positive is taken away from the environment following the behaviour. In the Johnny and father example, Johnny could have his ice cream taken away if he would misbehave. Negative punishment when applied skilfully in educational and parental situations only needs to happen actually a couple of times before the warning 'If you do not do X, I will take away Y' becomes a powerful tool in controlling behaviour.

What does this learning theory have to do with personality problems? Learning theory explains how certain very unhealthy behaviours are being maintained and triggered. For people with personality problems there is an abundant choice of self-defeating behaviours: self-harm, high-risk behaviours, addictive behaviours and oppositional behaviours. If we want to be able to help clients to change these, it is imperative that we understand the mainte-nance factors and can help clients to understand these as well.

Respondent learning

Respondent learning occurs when we make a connection between two events that originally were completely unconnected. The most famous example is of course Pavlov's experiments with his dogs. In this research the dogs received food (which caused them to salivate) whilst at the same time a buzzer would ring. After a number of repeats of this exercise, setting the buzzer off without the presentation of food would lead to saliva production in the dogs. In humans this mechanism operates in many anxiety problems where previous neutral events can trigger strong emotional reactions. (After having been in a car accident, the sound of cars makes a person nervous.)

The importance of respondent learning cannot be underestimated for the development of human misery. Here we learn reactions as a result of stimuli that have no reasonable connection with the manner in which we react. The example we frequently use in teaching about CBT is the following. Just imag-ine that a plane would crash on the building you are in now. Many people die a horrible death, you are in pain and while you are suffering you are terrified of dying and hear other people's screams of agony. While you are experi-encing that, your mind takes in everything from the surroundings: colours, smells and sounds. In a rather trivial way the mind can make connections between our fear of death and any of the elements of the environment that were observed. If you had been pinned to the floor on a bright red carpet, then the colour bright red might start to trigger feelings of anxiety. Reacting to these feelings of anxiety by avoiding situations with bright red activates the first learning principle (negative reinforcement).

Modelling

The modelling paradigm means we also learn from seeing others do things (Bandura, 1969, 1986), e.g. parents who smoke 'teach' their children that smoking is an acceptable thing to do.

In summary we learn to be miserable or behave badly as a result of how we interact with our environment. Consequences that are seen as positive will make the behaviours preceding them more likely. Negative feelings can be triggered by previously neutral events and stimuli when they have been combined once (for instance in a traumatic event) or many times (for instance being humiliated in a learning environment). Finally, we also learn to feel and do from what we see others feel and do.

EXAMPLE

If we take Rachel's learning history and review that with learning theory in mind, we can observe the following. In the left column we have listed events and patterns and in the right-hand column we review how learning theory applies.

Table 2.1

Rachel's history	A learning theory perspective
Rachel's mother was highly demanding and critical of everyone. Rachel told as an example that her mother would always carry with her a small supply of pristine white cloths and with delight she would run them across the tops of doors when visiting other people. They always came up dirty and mother would for days on end talk about the slovenly way of people and that she never would be caught out like that.	Mother MODELS criticising, high standards and 'catching people out'. Rachel follows in mother's footsteps by applying this to herself.
Mother strongly criticised Rachel, never praised. The criticism got less if Rachel worked very hard. Resting and engaging pleasure was strongly criticised and resulted in being given more tasks to do.	Rachel has learned that hard work results in negative reinforcement (less criticism). The ongoing criticism led to Rachel feeling very anxious during her childhood. She learned that by hard work she would 'forget' the anxiety (negative reinforcement).
When Rachel dared to question mother's rules or deviated from them mother would react in a punitive and nasty manner.	Rachel has learned that speaking her mind leads to punishment; she leaves it to others to decide her fate.

33

Cognitive theory

What we do and feel is also influenced by our thinking. If we are on our way to an important meeting and we are running late, how we feel and behave will depend on what we think.

We can identify various elements to our thinking.

Automatic thinking

This is exactly as it sounds: thinking that occurs outside our willpower, it just happens. We like to illustrate this to our students with the following example. Between 15 and 30 students are listening to the lecture and we ask them to close their eyes and just listen to the voice of the lecturer. The lecturer says the following: 'I want you to listen carefully to my voice. Shortly I will tap one of you on your right shoulder and that person needs to go to the front of the classroom and talk for five minutes about their first sexual experience.' We repeat this instruction several times while walking through the classroom. Of course no one ever gets tapped on the shoulder! There is always an abundance of automatic thoughts to choose from after the exercise. It is also immediately clear that most of the thoughts in the first instance are really automatic thoughts. Not one of the students woke up in the morning thinking: 'When I get asked today to talk for five minutes in front of the classroom about my first sexual experience, I will have these thoughts in my mind.' What the students think upon hearing the instruction is in the first instance purely automatic. A lot of our thinking is automatic like this and we let it pass by without giving it too much attention, unless the thoughts cause strong negative feelings, in which case we call these thoughts negative automatic thoughts (NATS). It is impossible to learn *not* to have NATS, but we can learn how we think about them. Popular NATS in the classroom exercise are:

- This is terrible, I will make a complete fool of myself.
- I can't stand this anxiety, it is intolerable.
- They shouldn't make us do this.

Crucial in how we feel about situations are not the NATS, but how we deal with our NATS.

Deliberate thinking (reasoning)

Once NATS are in our awareness we can use our deliberate thinking to deal with them. Depending on our training in thinking about NATS, our learning history and beliefs about the world and ourselves, we will either think in a way that promotes the validity of the NATS (and increases the negative feelings) or decreases the validity of the NATS and subsequently reduces the negative feelings.

Table 2.2

NATS	NATS Promotion	NATS Validity Reduction
This is terrible, I will make a complete fool of myself.	If I make a fool of myself, I will lose all respect, no one will like me anymore.	Well, it may be unpleasant, but terrible, certainly not. We are all students together and if I make a complete fool of myself that might lead to some interesting discussions.
I can't stand this anxiety, it is intolerable.	This anxiety will kill me, I have to leave, it is unbearable.	Feeling anxious is not pleasant, but I have felt anxious in the past and survived it unscathed!
The b******s, they shouldn't make us do this.	It is imperative that lecturers do not put students in difficult situations.	Certain learning experiences may be unpleasant, but that doesn't mean the lecturers should not do it.

Beliefs, core beliefs, attitudes and rules

Our NATS and deliberate thinking are guided by what we believe about ourselves, other people and the future as well as by the rules we apply to ourselves and others. Someone with a belief that 'life should be easy' would be inclined to have NATS of the 'it is intolerable' kind. Someone with a belief that others are potentially evil, may produce a NAT of the 'The b******s, they shouldn't make us do this' kind. In the literature there is in general a distinction between beliefs and core beliefs. The latter are more fundamental and sound really unconditional and absolute; while beliefs are often conditional and less absolute. Unhelpful beliefs are often present in categories about the self, other people and/or the future.

Table 2.3

	Belief	Core Belief
Self	In order to be a good person I need to do things to perfection.	I have to be perfect or I am a reject.
Others	People will only accept me if I do things to perfection.	Others are mean spirited and never forgive me my mistakes.
Future	Things will get better in the future if I can only achieve perfection.	The future is hopeless.

With 'rules', we mean rules for living. These are guiding principles about how the client demands that he/she should live or demands about other people's behaviour. Examples are:

- I always have to be fair.
- People should treat me with respect.
- Loyalty to the family comes above everything.
- People should give me what I want.

How we interpret what is happening to us dictates how we feel about a certain situation. Most of our interpretations are reasonably spot-on – we get it right.

However, especially in situations where there is no real right or wrong interpretation, our mind may go into 'thinking overdrive'. In CBT this is referred to as irrational thinking. This style of thinking is characterised by not being fact based, but based on the person's opinion and/or preference. This irrational thinking also leads to feeling bad and/or doing bad things. In other words, irrational thinking is not helpful because it is very 'unscientific' and does not help us to get what we want out of life.

Irrationality can occur in the automatic thinking, in deliberate thinking and in beliefs and core beliefs

In the following brief extract from a session we outline how the therapist interviews the client in such a way as to gain an understanding of how the learning principles and thinking principles apply to the client's problems.

T:	The next thing I would like to do today is to perhaps look at the list of problems we identified last time and then perhaps select one of those of which an example happened in the last week and talk about that specific example. Let us see if we can make sense of that. Would that be ok?
	Therapist comments: by examining a specific situation the therapist is able to get a glimpse at how learning and thinking principles apply.
Rachel:	Yes.
T:	The problems that we highlighted last week were working so hard that it makes you sad, snappy and aggressive with other people around you. Another problem that we identified was harsh self-criticism, which lead you also to become very sad and which resulted in you becoming very snappy and nagging with other people. You also mentioned that you have this belief that you are not good enough, which makes you feel quite bad about yourself. Did something happen in the last week regarding any of these problems?
Rachel:	We were having people over for supper on Tuesday. Tuesday is not really a great day anyway, as I have to pick the children up later on Tuesday because it is choir, so I left work at 2.30 and I dashed home wanting to get the place clean, really properly clean, and get started on the supper.
	Therapist's comments: client lists many tasks and uses the term 'really clean'; could this be evidence of high and unrelenting standards, possible core belief and rule for living.
T:	So you left work early and you then went home to give the place a proper clean. Right.
Rachel:	And to try and get the supper started. Anyway I managed to get the house clean and I started to prepare the vegetables and things and

then I completely lost track of time and I ended up being half an hour late for school picking the children up, which was so humiliating as they rang me on my mobile phone to find out where I was. I am never late and then I got the children in the car and got home. I was so cross with them.

T: You were cross with them.

Rachel: They were not doing anything, but I was cross with myself for being late. *(Client describes a busy day and subsequently engages in punishing herself for her efforts.)* Anyway I gave them their tea and got them in the bath. While they were in the bath I was doing the supper and put the supper in the oven and then went upstairs and got the children out of the bath. I put them to bed and then John came home and the guests arrived. I served the dinner, which was ok. They left and I went upstairs at the end of the evening and to my utter horror I had forgotten to let the children's bath water out. There was grey murky water where they had had the soap in there. It just looked disgusting with all the toys and everything. The guests had used the bathroom and they had seen it. I was mortified and then I went downstairs to talk to John about it and he said it didn't matter and clearly it did matter. It mattered to me and then we had a row.

Therapist's comments: there is some real evidence of unrelenting standards here and engaging in behaviour whereby client's hard work gets punished.

T: It was quite a big thing for you and he said it did not matter at all.

Rachel: He said they probably didn't notice and he said if they did notice then they knew that we had children and they had enjoyed the meal and that was all that was important. Well, it was not all that was important.

Therapist's comments: client demonstrates how much she is attached to her beliefs and how she 'punishes' the rational perspective of her husband.

Rachel: Anyway he ended up sleeping on the sofa, because I just went upstairs and shut the door because I did not even want to look at him. I was so humiliated, utterly mortified and he had no under-standing whatsoever just how bad it was. I had been cross with the children and I had not really enjoyed the supper because I had this nagging feeling that I had forgotten something and I could not think what it was that I had forgotten and everything was on the table and the dinner was ready and I had got the dessert there and everything. *(More evidence of unrelenting standards.)*

37

Examples of irrational thinking

Shoulding   This involves thinking in shoulds and musts: life should be fair; I have to have what I want: people should be nice to me; I have to be approved of by others.

Catastrophising   This is making mountains out of molehills. In life it is normal that things go wrong: we make mistakes, take a wrong turn, miss a train, arrive late for a meeting, are rejected for a job. Instead of seeing it as one of life's unfortunate and perhaps unpleasant/inconvenient or disappointing moments, we label it as a catastrophe, terrible or awful.

Self/other downing   We all make mistakes; we are all fallible human beings. When we apply this thinking error, we throw this fact of life out of the window. When noticing mistakes made by others we are inclined to draw conclusions about them as a person: Joe was late for a meeting, what a b*****d to show so little respect; I make some spelling mistakes, therefore I am a complete idiot.

Low frustration tolerancing   Here we overestimate the effect of events on us. We may say things like 'I can't stand this anymore', or words to that effect. We ignore the fact, that if we still can say that we can't stand something, we are still standing it!

All-or-nothing thinking   We see things in black and white categories. If our performance falls short of perfect, we see ourselves as total failures, or worthless. We may say things to ourselves like this: 'If I don't do it perfectly there's no point in doing it at all.'

Over-generalisation   We see a single negative event as a never-ending pattern of defeat, e.g. we use 'always' or 'never' words. An example of this might be: 'I never get anything right.'

Mental filter   We tend to pick out single negative details and dwell on them exclusively so that our vision of all reality becomes darkened, like the drop of ink that discolours the entire beaker of water. We say things like: 'I didn't have a moment's pleasure today.'

Disqualifying the positive   We reject positive experiences by insisting they 'don't count' for some reason or other (e.g. anyone can do that, that was easy). In this way we can maintain a negative belief even if it is contradicted by our everyday experiences.

Jumping to conclusions   We make a negative interpretation even though there is no evidence that convincingly supports this conclusion. This is an example of such a thinking error: 'Everyone is fed up with me.'

Magnification (catastrophising) or minimisation   We exaggerate the importance of things (such as our mistake or someone else's achievement) or we inappropriately shrink things until they appear tiny (our own desirable qualities or the other person's imperfections): 'I always fail my exams, while other people always pass the first time.'

Emotional/cognitive reasoning   We assume that our negative emotions necessarily reflect the way things really are: 'I feel it therefore it must be true'. The same goes for our thinking: 'I think it, therefore it must be true and important.'

Personalisation   We see ourselves as the cause of some negative external event, which in fact we were not primarily responsible for. Self-blaming can lead to anger at ourselves and feeling much worse. Blame is only possible if we intend something, otherwise it is unfortunate, or regretful, but should not lead to self-downing or guilt: 'If only I had paid more attention X would not have happened.'

Thinking, Behaving and Feeling

Thinking, behaving and feeling are connected. What we think influences how we feel and guides our behaviour. How we feel affects what we think and influences what we do. Our behaviour has an impact on how we feel and what we think. These three elements of humanity are loosely coupled systems: they influence each other in a reciprocal manner. Applying irrational thinking increases the likelihood of strong and unhealthy negative feelings and often promotes self-defeating behaviour.

Irrational thinking that does neither (no unhealthy negative feelings and no self-defeating behaviours) is of no interest to a cognitive behaviour therapist. We are not the thought police. It is people's right to think irrationally. If this irrational thinking leads to problem feelings and/or problem behaviours then CBT can get involved.

This leads to the question of which feelings are unhealthy and which are healthy. The first principle here is that not all negative feelings are unhealthy, nor are all positive feelings healthy in all circumstances.

To be grief-stricken when a loved one has died is a normal negative feeling in the first months up to a year after the person has passed away. To be still completely grief-stricken after five years is an unhealthy negative emotion. To be overwhelmed with grief when visiting the grave of a loved one, even five years after the death, is a healthy reaction. However, to go into complete emotional meltdown each time the name of the loved one is mentioned after five years is perhaps an unhealthy emotional reaction.

To be irritated when a friend arrives late for an appointment is a healthy negative emotion, but to be extremely angry is perhaps unhealthy.

In short there are a few parameters to consider. Does the situation warrant the *type* and *intensity* of the emotion? If we answer this with 'no', then the emotion can be considered an unhealthy negative one. Does the level, intensity or frequency of the emotion impact negatively on the person's life? If the answer is 'yes', then the emotion can be considered an unhealthy negative one.

We can put this in two lists, of unhealthy negative feelings and healthy negative feelings. It could be said that the aim of CBT is not to eradicate negative feelings but to assist clients to put them in proportion, from unhealthy negative to healthy negative.

Unhealthy Negative	Healthy Negative
Anxiety	Apprehension
Depression	Sadness
Anger	Irritation
Guilt	Remorse
Hurt	Disappointment
Shame/Embarrassment	Concern

RACHEL AS AN EXAMPLE

If we go back to Rachel and investigate how the thinking component of CBT applies to her, then the following picture emerges. When Rachel is confronted with tasks, her automatic thought is: 'That needs to be done', followed by 'I have to do it now'. Her deliberate thinking is around being careful and not making mistakes, how terrible a mistake would be, how terrible it would be if other people noticed. She also often says to herself that it is good that her mother is not seeing this as she would have something to say about it. When she makes mistakes she goes into full-blown self-downing. When she feels tired, the same thing happens. She still notices at times her own preference and wishes in situations, but will rarely put them forward, for fear that others might not approve. She avoids conflict and aggravation almost at all cost. The emotions she experiences are depression, anxiety and guilt.

The example of the bathwater is a typical example of how strong the adherence is to their irrational thinking processes of people with a personality problem (Rachel had been diagnosed as an avoidant personality disorder by the referring psychiatrist). Even when her husband points out factual evidence that her perspective (the friends were shocked and horrified at the bathwater is wrong (everyone had a good evening and the guests expressed their gratitude), she still persists in holding on to what she thinks is her reality.

The examples highlight that the same learning principles and cognitive process apply to people with personality disorders as apply to everyone else. The difference is one of rigidity. People with a diagnosis of personality disorder are much more rigid in their behaviour and thinking patterns. It is as if they have once found a solution to a problem and they keep on using that same solution even though the problems/circumstances have changed.

Bella very well demonstrates this. She is a 27-year-old client who has received a diagnosis of borderline personality disorder. When discussing an episode of self-harming behaviour (Bella made cuts with a razor blade on her leg) she was asked if she could think of different ways of dealing with the feeling of depression and despair that prompted the self-harm. During the next 30 minutes Bella came up with the following strategies:

- I could have cut my arms.
- I could have burned myself.
- I could have banged my head against the wall.
- I could have used needles.
- I could have started an argument with my boyfriend so he would have had to hit me.

The behaviour is different, but the type of solution is the same.

The explanation for this rigidity in thinking and behaving can be hypothesised to stem from three sources (Livesley, 2003):

- Genetic predisposition.
- Persistent reinforcement of certain actions and thinking processes.
- Over-learning of certain behavioural and thinking processes.

It is important for cognitive behaviour therapists working with clients having personality difficulties to remember that the processes and content are very similar to those of other clients, but that these clients' perseverance against odds with their unhelpful patterns is formidable.

Contemplating on Theory

We started off by saying that nothing is as practical as a good theory. Applying CBT as a psychological therapy in working with personality disorder is more and beyond the application of a set of specific interventions. The complexity of personality disorder makes it beneficial that psychological therapists can understand the theoretical underpinnings of their actions (and of clients' actions!).

Understanding Check

Things you should be able to do after reading this chapter:

1 Explain the core components of CBT.
2 Explain principles such as positive and negative reinforcement, operant learning and respondent learning as they no longer hold any secrets for you.
3 Identify your own preferred thinking errors.
4 Explain the various levels of cognitive activity and how they impact on human behaviour.

3

THE PROCESS OF CBT: FROM SYMPTOMS TO PROBLEMS AND GOALS, MOVING ON TO FORMULATION

In this chapter you will learn about:

- How CBT is structured for people with personality difficulties.
- The chronological steps a CBT therapist needs to take to conduct 'good' CBT.
- The importance of good problem and goal definitions.
- The meaning and use of topographical and functional analyses.
- The link between formulation and the functional and topographical analyses.

Introduction

CBT is typically a short-term treatment in which the therapist helps the client to learn more effective methods of dealing with troubling thoughts, feelings and behaviour. It also is a problem-oriented therapy that both addresses the situational difficulties that may have provoked anxious or depressive episodes and the underlying cognitive problems that may relate to the pathogenesis of emotional disorders. Having said this, we have to add to this statement that it is correct for problems with anxiety and depression of mild to moderate severity. When the problems are severe and long-standing, when there are co-morbid issues and when the clients live in areas of high socio-economic deprivation even CBT treatments will last longer. The guidelines for length of treatment of the United Kingdom's Institute for Health and Clinical Excellence vary from eight (anxiety) to 20 (depression) sessions. For clients with personality difficulties treatment will take longer. Periods ranging from 18 months (Linehan, 1993) to three years (Giesen-Bloo et al., 2006) are mentioned. We often find ourselves in heated debates with service managers wanting to set up short-term CBT personality disorder services. We have to point out that to do such a thing would be to instruct a plastic surgeon to do the work with a pocked knife in the middle of the road. We have the evidence that CBT can work for clients with personality problems, but there is no such thing as a free lunch. In order to run a CBT-based service for personality disorders, it would be unethical to limit the amount of time spent with clients to less then two years of at least weekly sessions. Treatment efficacy can be enhanced by adding skills based group CBT and opportunities to have periods of more than one session per week.

People with personality difficulties often enter therapy against their will. They enter our consulting rooms on the strong recommendation of others and at other times seeing a therapist is mandatory. This does not endear the client to the therapist. Often clients come to therapy ready to disprove that they need therapy.

Structuring treatment and treatment sessions is extremely important in working with clients who have personality problems. The challenge is to combine adhering to evidence-based structures with increasing and maintaining clients' motivation. People with personality problems often have rigid ways in which they want others to behave towards them. A proposed structure of therapy and/or therapy sessions often clashes with this rigidity. Therapists will have to combine the structured way of working of CBT and dealing with these inter-personal challenges.

We distinguish the following phases in treatment:

- Pre-therapy phase: assessing the client's readiness for psychological therapy and increasing the client's readiness.
- Informing phase: data gathering, assessment, socialising to the CBT model, composing a formulation, feeding back the formulation to the client, designing and deciding on an intervention plan.
- Change phase: client and therapist work making and maintaining changes.

Pre-Therapy

We are often amazed by the implicit acceptance of many therapists that they *know* their clients have problems. The rights clinicians give themselves in interviewing clients astounds us.

A typical process of therapy starts with the therapist bombarding the client with a tidal wave of questions. It pays to have a think about this and to accept that there is a pre-therapy phase in which we have to elicit permission from the client to embark on an assessment process. In this eliciting phase the therapist's goal is to make the clients curious about their situation, so curious that they also want to embark on the assessment process in order to find out what it is that causes their misery. The pre-therapy/eliciting phase can last five minutes (very unlikely in clients with personality problems) or a number of sessions (very likely). It all depends on clients' perspective on their situation, e.g. the stages of change (see Chapter 7 'Engagement Strategies') they find themselves in. For a client in a stage where he/she is convinced there are no real problems the process might take longer than for a client ready for active change.

In this pre-therapy phase the task of the therapist is to get the client ready for participation in an assessment. This is extremely important in working with clients having personality difficulties. Because of the rigidity of their behaviour and thinking patterns, they find it difficult to see that the negative feelings they experience and/or maladaptive behaviour they engage in have anything to do with how they lead their lives.

Gabriel was diagnosed by his psychiatrist as having an obsessive-compulsive personality disorder. He was a successful businessman and had been so for years. He worked seven days per week and on most days he would spend more then 12 hours working. Gabriel had not sought help for his OCD behaviour (not being able to stop if something was unfinished) but for his deep sense of gloom and doom. In other words his style of doing his job had made him depressed. It took an experienced therapist many sessions to help Gabriel understand that working hard and in the obsessive manner, contributed strongly to the development of depression. The first step in this process was to get Gabriel to be curious about why he was getting depressed so he would agree with a comprehensive assessment to find out how the problem started and how it is maintained.

During the pre-therapy phase there is often a discrepancy between the clinician's implicit perception (the client has been referred to me therefore there must be some real problems) and the client's perception (there is in fact not much wrong with me and if there is it is not my fault). During this phase the clinician has to work at increasing clients' curiosity regarding their personal situation.

This phase often resembles on the surface a casual chat; what is needed, however, is skilled motivational interviewing (see Chapter 7). Table 3.1 is an excerpt of a first interview with a client with a referral diagnosis of histrionic personality disorder with depressive features. The first goal is to elicit from the client signs that she recognises problems and is concerned about them, while in the meantime not reducing her self-esteem and sense of self-efficacy. The therapist applies motivational interviewing to get the client to a point where she has 'discovered' sufficient personal problems that warrant a further assessment.

Informing Phase

This phase consists of two parts. The first part is where client and therapist collect information about the client's situation, while in the second phase the therapist feeds back this information to the client. During this phase, the client has become a bit curious about his/her personal situation. ('Perhaps it is worthwhile to chat with this person – at least he doesn't preach to me!') Client and therapist start an active quest for information. It is very important that the client as well as the therapist finds it useful and necessary to gather this information. With the information that is gathered the client can decide

Table 3.1

Interview	Comments
Therapist: Annabelle, thanks for coming to see me. We do have about 50 minutes to talk about things that you would like to talk about.	Open question, with an attempt to set an agenda.
Annabelle: There is nothing I want to talk about.	Statements like this are often indicative, especially at a first session of client's scepticism
Therapist: So there is nothing you would like to talk about?	
Annabelle: No.	
Therapist: Right. So you have come here today because …	
Annabelle: Only because I was sent here. By everyone [screams] they are all ganging up against me, my husband, my GP, even my children, they all say I am the problem.	Strong emotional outburst, given the content, indicative of well established 'defence' systems against acknowledging personal problems.
Therapist: Everyone is ganging up against you, you were made to come here? Can you tell me a bit more about that?	
Annabelle: Well, my GP, my family and everybody think that I should be here [calmer].	
Therapist: So your GP and your family all think you should be here.	Reflections
Annabelle: Oh, yes. Everyone thinks there is something wrong with me.	
Therapist: Everyone thinks there is something wrong with you.	
Annabelle: Mm.	
Therapist: From what you say it sounds like you completely disagree with them?	In motivational interviewing terms this is an overshooting: the reflection is in a direction (there is no problem) that the therapist does not want to pursue, but is made so strong the client may feel tempted to disagree.
Annabelle: Well, you just have to get on with life, don't you? I mean you know. Some things are good and some things are bad. You just have to get on with it; it doesn't mean that there is something wrong with you. Does it?	
Therapist: So you are saying, that it sounds like a philosophy of your life that whatever life throws at you, you just have to get on with life.	Therapist reflects the intent and meaning behind the spoken words.
Annabelle: That's what my mother used to say – yes. I mean that some people just have more bad stuff than others really, don't they?	Seems like client had had a good training in not acknowledging problems.
Therapist: So getting on with life is very important with you?	In motivational interviewing terms this is a positive restructuring, focusing on client's positive intention.
Annabelle: It just is that it is really tiring though, isn't it. Well, that doesn't mean there is something wrong with you – does it? If you just feel tired, well just being tired isn't something wrong with you – is it?	Which then leads to the client talking about experienced problems.

Table 3.1 *(Continued)*

Interview	Comments
Therapist: So you are saying on the one hand you believe firmly that your family is completely 200% in the wrong by saying that there is something wrong with you and on the other hand you are saying tiredness is an issue. Can you tell me some more about that?	
Annabelle: I'm just tired; that is all – just always tired. Really weary – you know!	
Therapist: Really weary and tired?	Getting the client to talk more about experienced problems.
Annabelle: I never wake up feeling not tired.	

whether there is reason to be concerned about his/her situation or there is nothing to worry about.

A good starting point to collect information is to get a helicopter view of the problem issues. The therapist needs an overview of the client's present engagement in the problem behaviour: how often, how much, how intense and how long. The therapist needs to use the six Ws to structure questions:

What is the problem?
Where does the problem occur?
With whom is the problem better or worse?
When does the problem happen?
What happens before the problem occurs?
What happens as a result of the problem?

In order to get a clear picture of the issues involved it is important to collect some examples of what exactly happens when the problem occurs. We call this a 'topographical analysis' and the model we use for this is called SORCC (Stimulus Organism Response Consequence Contingency).

The SORCC maintenance cycle

The SORCC maintenance cycle is a helpful system to understand how reinforcement and other learning theory paradigms play a role in the maintenance of problems (Goldfried, 2003; Nezu and Lombardo, 2004; Eells, 2006; Sturmey, 2007).

Stimulus
This involves a description of the situation that triggers the problem or the situation in which the problem occurs. This would involve issues such as places, times and people.

Organism

This involves the client's internal reaction to the situation: cognitions, feelings and physiology. Of course these three elements may 'fire' in a certain sequence, which is also important to note.

Responses

These are the behaviours the client engages in as a result of the 'O' reaction. What we often see is that what happens in 'O' is perceived by the client as unpleasant and they see the behaviour they engage in as the only option to escape the unpleasantness. We also often see cognitions emerge that give 'permission' to engage in unhelpful behaviour. It is important to recognise that the 'emotions–cognitions–physiology' cycle can go round several times before the client engages in the problem behaviour.

This is how it worked for Valerie:

They did not want me there (cognition)→ Sadness (emotion)→ They should not make me sad (c)→ Anger (e)→ I have to show them how badly they treat me (c)→ Agitation (physiology)→ If I really hurt myself they will be sorry.

Consequences

Here the actual result of the behaviour is described and interpreted from a learning theory perspective. What is the result of the behaviour and is it a reinforcing or punishing consequence? As a general rule problem behaviours that continue to happen 'need' reinforcement otherwise they would be extinguished. Often clients find it difficult to understand the validity of consequences (e.g. is the consequence rewarding or not) and that is because they have a time frame that is too long. When we asked Valerie what happened after her self-harm (cutting her face with a razor blade) she said she felt horrible, guilty and disgusted with herself. When we then took her mind back to the action of slashing her face and asked what was going through her mind and how she was feeling during and immediately after the cutting, she said that she thought about how much this would show her friends how badly they had behaved towards her and that she felt an intense surge of energy go through her body. For the maintenance cycle we really are interested in the consequences closest to the problem behaviour, not what happened after one hour, but what happened after one minute! Immediate consequences are far more important in influencing the behaviours they follow than longer-term consequences.

Contingencies

The other elements of the SORCC paradigm refer to elements that occur in a certain chronology: the situation, the person's internal reaction, the behavioural response and the consequences that follow the behaviour. 'Contingencies' does not refer to a specific element, but to the relationship between two elements: the behavioural response and the consequences. From a learning perspective this relationship is extremely important. A consequence that occurs 100 per cent of the time in the presence of the behaviour and never when the behaviour is *not* present, will be very effective in getting the behaviour established in the person's repertoire for as long as the 100 per cent connection occurs. Behaviour-consequences connections of the 100 per cent kind are, however, not very resistant against 'unlearning' the behaviour. When used to 100 per cent connection, the behaviour will be rapidly terminated when the connection no longer occurs. The story is very different for a more intermittent and variable link between behaviour and consequence. Here the person has learned that there is a chance the consequence may occur, so if it does not materialise for several occurrences of the behaviour, the person will still persist. This is what gamblers do and this is what has hooked us on watching television. In both cases if you persist long enough you will win or watch something good on TV!

SORCC EXAMPLE

For this example we visit Claire. She is a woman in her mid-forties. She has received a diagnosis from her psychiatrist as 'borderline personality disorder with histrionic features'. One of her problem behaviours was engaging in high-risk behaviour (cutting, fast driving and closing eyes, going home with complete strangers). In this session we tried to establish the function of her cutting herself. (In the end we distinguished three types: despair cutting (= being in a complete upset state and just wanting 'it' to stop); entertainment cutting (= cutting as an activity that entertains); and communication cutting (= a message for family and friends). In order to achieve clarity regarding the various forms of cutting it was necessary to discuss the cutting in detail with Claire and to ask her to complete a detailed diary.

Stimulus:
Being alone and no urgent tasks to do
Organism:
Ruminating about past mistakes, disappointments, real and imagined sleights from other people, leading to

catastrophising thoughts → despair and anxiety

demanding thoughts → anger

(Continued)

Being bored leading to craving for the adrenaline rush of cutting →
thoughts about doing it.

images of being cared for and nurtured → thoughts of doing it.

Behaviour:
Cutting arms, legs, stomach with a sharp razor blade, slow evenly spaced
long cuts.

Consequences:
Short term: adrenaline rush, 'the beauty of the blood', removal of boredom
and despair (relief), 'positive' revenge thoughts ('now they will know how
bad they treated me!').

Longer term: expressed concern by others, loathing of self, loathing by
others.

Contingencies: all consequences are intermittent and client has noticed
that lately 'more and deeper' cutting is needed to produce the same
consequences. The consequences are a mix of positive reinforcements
(positive revenge thoughts, the beauty of the blood, adrenaline rush) and
negative reinforcements (removal of boredom, anxiety and despair).

Using the SORCC paradigm explains the vicious cycle Claire was caught up
in: cognitions and emotions that were perceived as negative were effectively
removed by the cutting, but satiation resulted in an increased need for more
(intense) cutting to produce the same reinforcements. Having uncovered such
a SORCC sequence is very helpful in establishing an agenda of further issues
to explore: the client's selective attention to negative events from her past: her
tendency to catastrophise, her demanding thinking and her boredom. Each of
these can be explored in connection to other elements of the SORCC and
historically. This eventually will lead to a complete picture in the format of the
BASIC-ID (Behaviour Affect Sensations Interpersonal Cognitive Imagery
Drugs & Alcohol).

Self-monitoring to assist SORCC
John identified as one of his issues feeling really depressed and as a result of
this not doing things he normally needed or liked to do. John also mentioned
drinking too much and at times getting very angry and aggressive towards
family.

First the therapist interviews the client to get a retrospective diary of last
week's problem behaviour. A good way to do this is to use a flip chart and use
the format shown in Table 3.2 as a guideline.

Table 3.2

Day	Morning	Afternoon	Evening/Night
Monday			
Tuesday			
Wednesday			
Thursday			
Friday			
Saturday			
Sunday			

Example of self-monitoring

Table 3.3

Day	Morning	Afternoon	Evening/Night
Monday	Depression: 8 out of 10 Avoidance: did not go to work	Depression: 8 out of 10 Avoidance: did not go to work Drinking: three cans of beer	Depression: 6 out of 10 Avoidance: did not do anything, watched TV Drinking: bottle of wine Aggression: shouted at kids
Tuesday	Depression: 8 out of 10	Depression: 3 out of 10	Depression: 4 out of 10 Avoidance: did not do anything Drinking: 2 cans of beer and a bottle of wine

The therapist then starts either with yesterday or with yesterday a week ago, and works day by day through a week. The therapist takes every day in three parts. The question to ask is: 'How often/much did you do it on Monday morning?' Get the client to be specific. If the client cannot remember, then the therapist can mention a very low figure and a very high figure. The client then will feel that he/she can safely mention his/her best guess.

This is something that can be done in a first session. It can be followed by focusing on one or more problem incidents that client or therapist would like to focus on in the form of a topographical analysis (TA). A TA is a detailed analysis of one problem occurrence. The aim is to uncover specific triggers (internal or external) for the problem and relevant consequences (internal or external).

TA

If we want to know how problem behaviours, problem emotions, problem thoughts, problematic environmental reactions and physiological responses interact together then we need to construct several topographical analyses. A topographical analysis or TA for short is a detailed description of what actually happens during a problem moment. This is mapping out a specific problem occurrence. The most basic way of doing this is in the format of SORCC description shown in Table 3.4.

Table 3.4

Antecedents		Problem Behaviours (R)	Consequences & Contingencies (CC)
External (S)	Internal (O)		
Internal: Thoughts, feelings, sensations		What the client did to go from ANTECEDENTS to CONSEQUENCES.	Internal: Thoughts, feelings, sensations
Personal Behaviour			Personal Behaviour
External: situations, times, people			External: situations, times, people

A TA is helpful in uncovering which antecedents are too difficult to deal with for the client without the problem behaviour and for which feelings or behaviours the client needs the problem behaviour.

Examples

From the TA in Table 3.5, the therapist can hypothesise that for the problem of depression and avoidance the client finds it impossible to resist the thought 'I can't cope' and/or the sensation of tiredness. For the 'shouting' problem the therapist can hypothesise that the client can only reduce his frustration/irritation by raising his voice and acting aggressively. If these hypotheses are confirmed by further TAs and self-observations the therapy goals become obvious: cognitive restructuring of the 'toxic' thoughts; learning to ignore 'toxic' thoughts as guidance for behaviour and learning stress/irritation reduction by non aggressive communication methods. Armed with some TAs the therapist can now compose a functional analysis (FA).

Table 3.5

Antecedents (S & O)	Problem (R)	Consequences (CC)
Feelings: lethargic, tired; Thinking: 'I can't cope'	Depressed and avoiding going to work	Internal: Thoughts: 'At least nothing can go wrong here.'; feelings: relief, lethargic, tired.
Personal Behaviour: lying in bed at 8 a.m.		Personal Behaviour: lying in bed
External: in the morning, having to go to work		External: still in bed
Antecedents	Problem	Consequences
Internal: Thoughts: I can't stand it any longer; feelings: irritation; sensations: tense	Shouting at the children	Internal: Thoughts: they should not have done that; I am a bad person for shouting at them; feelings: briefly reduced frustration; sensations: bit energetic
Personal Behaviour: watching TV on the couch		Personal Behaviour: walking away to my room with a drink
External: situations: in the lounge at home; times: late afternoon evenings; people: kids asking me to do a game with them		External: situations: alone

A functional analysis aims to uncover the *function* of the problem behaviour. Functions can be defined as enabling someone to achieve something desirable or avoid something undesirable. In other words a function of behaviour can be:

- Avoiding negative feelings (when feeling depressed staying in the warm and cosy bedroom); aversive thoughts and feelings (self-harming to avoid feeling very depressed and thoughts about being bad); situations and people.
- Having access to positive feelings (drinking alcohol to relax); behaviours that are seen as positive (drinking alcohol to be able to socialise); and access to situations and people.

The function of problem behaviours can be understood by carefully examining what triggers the behaviour and what is the result of the behaviour.

The first quest is to find out what happens before the problem behaviour. By scanning carefully a number of occasions in which the client engaged in problem behaviour the therapist may be able to locate 'eliciting factors' of the problem behaviour. These factors are situations, places, people, emotions and thoughts, which through a learning process have become powerful enough to elicit certain behaviours; in this case the problem behaviour.

In which situations does the problem behaviour occur? In some situations the problem behaviour may be appropriate (drinking two glasses of wine during a meal) but in other situations the same behaviour may be inappropriate (drinking two glasses of wine in the morning before going to work). The therapist has to find out what in the situation makes the client decide to engage in the problem behaviour. By doing so the therapist prepares for the next step. By 'forcing' the client to explain why he/she did drink or smoke, the client has to expand on thoughts and feelings that were involved.

Clients 'use' the problem behaviour to get rid of a negative emotion or to improve on a positive emotion in order to feel even better. By analysing the problem behaviour diaries the therapist can compile a list of emotions that the client deals with by 'indulging' in the problem behaviour. The implication for treatment is that the client needs to learn different strategies in dealing with these negative emotions.

We also can recognise thinking strategies that are 'problem behaviour inhibitors' and thinking styles that are of the 'permission-to-do-it' kind. Thoughts that inhibit problem solving are of the kind: 'This is going to be very difficult'; 'I am not sure if it is even worth trying to solve the problem'. Permission-giving thoughts are of the kind (for a problem drinker): 'I'll just go to the pub to have a chat with the mates'.

What does the person **expect** to achieve through the problem behaviour and what is **actually** achieved? People engage in certain behaviours because they make decisions that engaging in this behaviour will bring them something they want or believe they need. What people expect of certain behaviours is not always what actually will happen. For instance, problem drinkers may drink and expect to become less depressed; but drinking alcohol increases feelings of depression. The drinker experiences this effect, but does not conclude that his/her expectancy is wrong. The client concludes that he/she has not been drinking enough alcohol and that given persistence the depression will go. Expectancies of effects and actual effects of the problem behaviour are extremely important. Behaviour is controlled by its reinforcing consequences. In the case of problem behaviours we see that behaviours are controlled by the expected positive consequences even when in reality they do not occur.

In examining clients' experiences the therapist has to differentiate between the expected consequences and the actual consequences. Expected consequences can be very powerful in controlling behaviour. This explains the fact that people continue with the problem behaviour despite the fact that in reality short-term and long-term consequences are negative, but the expectancy of short-term consequences is positive.

Which behavioural, cognitive and/or emotional goals can be achieved with the problem behaviour? The therapist has to analyse the TAs very carefully and check which behavioural, cognitive and/or emotional goals can be achieved with the problem behaviour. The behaviour may have become a coping strategy for the client in dealing with certain difficult situations. Using the problem behaviour to achieve this (either in reality or as an expected achievement) is using a sort of short cut. For example, if using cocaine gives energy and courage to play on the stock market and be successful as an investment broker then this is using a short cut. Good rest and thinking one's feelings of anxiety through would get the same result but would take longer and require more effort.

Sometimes other people in the client's environment provide the client with a desirable or reinforcing consequence. The problem behaviour elicits responses from a spouse, a friend or a parent, which reinforces the addiction.

(Problem behaviour) history
Part of the functional analysis is to put the problem behaviour in a historical context. The following questions may need answering:

- When did the client start engaging in the problem behaviour?
- Which rules and regulations were connected to the problem behaviour?
- Which models did the client have regarding the behaviour?
- When did the behaviour become problematic?
- Are there problematic circumstances connected with the period in which the behaviour became problematic?

It also may be helpful to make a chronological time line of the behaviour and to make a retrospective overview of the last couple of years regarding the problem behaviour.

Especially with clients who have long-standing problems it may pay to go beyond the problem history and aim for a comprehensive historical analysis.

A functional analysis focuses on one problem area, while a formulation is a holistic theory about the emergence of all the problems and the interaction and maintenance of all the problems. In the example of Ann, we can imagine that in order to 'escape' her sense of being a failure she worked as hard as she could, resulting in depression and irritability. The marital conflicts increase the depression and irritation. It will be important to make a functional analysis of each of the problems and subsequently find the connection points between the various functional analyses.

In a formulation the therapist links the various problems and defines their relationships. At the same time each problem needs to be understood within the context of a functional analysis.

A formulation comprises of the main problems that make life difficult and explains how they are linked together. It helps to understand which problem issues are more or less central, e.g. which problems are causing the others and which are more peripheral. If a problem is strongly linked to stress and feeling irritable then treatment would need to teach the client to be able to reduce tension and irritation *and* to learn to tolerate these feelings without engaging in the self-defeating behaviours.

The BASIC-ID (Lazarus, 1981) is a model that is very helpful in composing formulations. The task of the therapist is to get information about the elements of the BASIC-ID in order to understand how the client 'learned' to have the problems they have.

Designing a detailed formulation that will guide the treatment plan is especially important in working with personality difficulties, as their problems are often complex and long-standing. What makes composing a detailed formulation also important is that these clients' reactions (behavioural, emotional and cognitive) to life's events are 'different'. This difference could be in intensity, frequency and duration, but also the quality of the reaction could be different.

An example of this was Valerie's explanation of a period of serious self-harming. When discussing it with her, the therapist's thinking was along the lines of 'self-harm fuelled by psychological despair'. However, when the therapist discussed with her in detail what she was thinking during this period of self-harm, she did not mention despair, but a desire for revenge. 'I will show the world that it owes me something, they can't treat me like this, they will be forever sorry if they see what I have done.'

Another client, who had killed his parents, surprised us when he explained his feelings and thoughts during the act of killing them. The expectancy would be that the client had been angry when killing his parents and again this client surprised us by saying that he felt sad when killing his parents. Sad, because he loved his parents, but he could not allow them to continue to disappoint him, as he would have stopped loving them. Killing them was his way of protecting his love for them and that made him sad.

As psychological therapists we may have a range of forms and question-naires to get information on the elements of the BASIC-ID, but this needs to be fine-tuned by careful interviewing and questioning.

We discuss the 'how' of the questioning and interviewing in Chapter 7, but here we would like to discuss the 'what'. Often students ask us 'What should I focus on?'; 'What are topics that I should pay attention to?' These questions are impossible to answer in a generic way. We would suggest focusing attention on problems (behaviours, emotions, cognitions, other people's behaviour) as defined by the client (and sometimes relevant others) and follow this up with a detailed investigation using the BASIC-ID model.

With Valerie the interview developed as follows (at the moment of the start of the extract we are 15 minutes into the session).

T:	From what you told me it seems like you have had a week with many difficulties.
Valerie:	You can say that again, it has been absolutely horrible, I have been completely consumed with despair, it just feels like everything and everyone is against me….
T:	Despair, you say – could you tell me when you experienced this despair strongest in the last week? (*Therapist uses client's most emotive word to start exploring the issues.*)
Valerie:	Yes, despair: being criticised at work, my friends going out without me, the car-repair bill was horrendously high, not having enough money to go on holiday where I want to go – it was just a horrible week.
T:	And when during the last week did you experience this despair strongest? (*Therapist 'ignores' client's list of issues for the moment – these will be explored later.*)
Valerie:	Well, it was Friday evening and I was at home – that is when I really felt it and when I started cutting with the razor blade.
T:	So Friday evening you felt really desperate and started cutting – what time was that and what were you doing before you started cutting? (*Therapist has uncovered one link, between self-labelled despair and the behaviour of cutting; further exploration regarding time and other behaviours.*)
Valerie:	It was around nine in the evening and I had been drinking gin and thinking about how badly people had treated me, especially my friend who went out on a karaoke night without me.
T:	Nine in the evening and you had been drinking gin and were thinking about how badly people treated you, especially your friends? (*Therapist uses active listening and pursuing the BASIC-ID.*)
	(*Continued*)

(Continued)

Valerie: Yes, they invited me to go with them to a karaoke night this Friday, but I did not feel like going and they still went – can you believe it, they completely rejected and humiliated me. They were having fun, while I was sitting alone at home. That really made me mad, so I thought I will show you what you have done to me and started cutting. Now they will be sorry to have abandoned me [crying]. *(This gives the therapist quite a bit of information of issues to pursue – it seems what the client has labelled as despair also had elements of anger in it and the cognitions are clearly focused on revenge.)*

By following the BASIC-ID elements for a number of problems, the therapist will get a clear idea of the nature of the client's problems.

Behaviour

Under this category the therapist tries to categorise the problem behaviours of the client *and* relevant pro-social behaviours. It is important to know intensity, frequency and duration of the relevant behaviours. Which behaviours are relevant in this context is dictated by the presenting problems of the client and context issues. For instance, the behaviours of a client working in an upmarket retail store, who uses many swear-words and abusive language will be understood differently compared to the behaviour of a client who spends most of his time in a semi-criminal and violent environment. In the first situation the behaviour is maladaptive and might get the client fired from his job and in the second situation it may be a survival strategy for the client.

The development of the (problem) behaviours is also reviewed here, as well as skills deficits. When it comes to skills deficits, it is important to distinguish between ability and performance. A client may know how to express positive feelings, but may never do this.

Affect

Frequency, duration and intensity of negative as well as positive feelings may provide important information regarding the client's problems; sometimes an excess of negative emotion *is* the problem. The link between affect and cognitions is an important one. Sometimes clients talk about feeling anxious and when we discuss their thinking the thoughts reflect anger. As psychological therapists we then have to untangle this. People with personality problems often experience a variety of feelings at any given time and it is imperative to get a clear picture. As a psychological therapist we need to understand what the emotions are and how they are driven by cognitions.

Sensations

Under sensations we would list physical experiences of the client, such as appetite, hunger, sleep and energy levels. It is important to investigate what the sensations are that exactly occur at problem moments and how they influence the problem. Sometimes, sensations experienced are the problem for the client (upset stomach, sweating) and then using the BASIC-ID paradigm will be helpful in understanding the links with thoughts, behaviour.

Interpersonal

Here it is important to review the client's interpersonal relationships, but also the potential for interpersonal relationships. Living as a foreigner in an overseas country without speaking the local language and no other English-speaking people within 500 miles limits the possibility of interpersonal relationships. This person may be highly skilled in interpersonal skills and really use each opportunity to connect with others, but there are no opportunities. Another person may live in an environment with a rich potential for interpersonal relationships, but does not have the skills to make use of the opportunities.

Cognitions

Here relevant cognitions and cognitive processes will be reviewed. It is not only the content of the cognitions, but also the way of processing. So here we have habitual negative automatic thoughts, rules for living, beliefs and core beliefs, as well as process issues such as rumination and selective attention.

The therapist would review here content of cognitions (negative automatic thoughts, beliefs or core beliefs) that facilitate problem behaviours and block pro-social behaviours.

A belief that other people are out to get you and put you down will 'promote' behaviours intended to defend the client against attacks like this (never admitting mistakes, always cover up mistakes, strive for perfection) and may lead to an avoidance of interaction with others (not using social skills).

Imagery

Images can often play a crucial role in the development and maintenance of problems. Clients with traumatic experiences can often see these events replaying in their mind over and over again. For clients with borderline personality disorder the hypothesised abandonment by loved ones is often played out in images; while people with a paranoid personality style can clearly visualise their loved one's infidelities.

Drugs and alcohol

Current and past use of substances may play a role in the maintenance or may have played a role in the development of the problems.

The BASIC-ID does not include a historical component, but we see this as an important part of the formulation. We call this a 'historical analysis'. Basically the therapist wants to understand how the client learned the maladaptive thinking and behaving style and for this a detailed history may need to be taken. If the client is prepared to do some work between sessions, then he/she can work on a 'time line', whereby for each year the client describes which bad events happened and which good events occurred.

Part of a historical analysis may be a history of medical emergencies and hospitalisations for clients with borderline personality difficulties. For clients with anti-social personality disorder difficulties or psychopathy, a list of criminal convictions may be reviewed.

BASIC-ID EXAMPLE

We will again take Claire and use her presentation as an example of understanding her by using the BASIC-ID paradigm.

Historical Analysis

Claire had experienced a very abusive childhood. An uncle sexually abused her for many years and did so in a cruel and denigrating manner. Her parents were cold and distant, not showing any affection. Their interaction with their children was an instrumental one: the children had to work hard on the farm and any performance lower then expected resulted in heavy criticism. Claire did attend school haphazardly and did not achieve any qualifications. She started self-harming at age 12 and engaging in high-risk behaviours at age 19.

Behaviour

There are a number of behavioural excesses: shouting demands aggressively, self-harm and high-risk behaviours. There are more behavioural deficits: expressing positive and negative feelings, making requests; problem solving; self-management (planning pleasurable and satisfying activities).

Affect

There is an excess of anxiety, despair and anger and a deficit of contentment, happiness and satisfaction.

(Continued)

Sensations

Claire mentions sensations of lethargy and fatigue as slowing her down to do things.

Interpersonal

Claire is married and has two children. She lives in a small village, she knows many people and people know her, but she has no close friends. When people are friendly to her, she calls them her best friend and expects/demands them to be there for her 24/7, which results in many disappointments and interpersonal problems. As mentioned under 'behaviour' she lacks a series of interpersonal skills.

Cognitions

Claire 'uses' the cognitive process of ruminating frequently. The content of her ruminations indicates an excessive attentional focus on personal mistakes, disappointing behaviour by others, things going wrong, negative emotional states and negative physical experiences. She has a tendency to catastrophise and overgeneralise. Her 'rules' for living are: I should get what I want from life and it is pointless to try if things don't happen by themselves. Beliefs and core beliefs were around abandonment (whatever happens, people I need will abandon me), entitlement (I should get what I need and want) and mistrust (people can't be trusted).

Imagery

Claire is plagued by nightmares and intrusive images about the abuse from her uncle.

Drugs and Alcohol

Claire over-indulges in alcohol, infrequently, but when she does it triggers engaging in high-risk behaviours.

In summary

Childhood abuse and a harsh upbringing instilled beliefs about mistrust, abuse and abandonment in Claire. In combination with being very unskilled in communication skills this results in fraught interpersonal relationships. This means that Claire seldom gets what she wants from life and other people. This missing out has now led to an entitlement belief, which means that she perceives all interpersonal relationships as a test for this belief. She dictates interpersonal relationships and interprets others not wanting to go along with that as abuse and abandonment. When she perceives abandonment or abuse, she reacts with

(Continued)

strong negative feelings of either anger or anxiety. Engaging in high-risk behaviours is Claire's strategy to reduce the impact of these negative feelings. She has only excessive drinking of alcohol as an alternative to high-risk behaviours in dealing with negative affect.

The formulation will indicate what the client will need to learn in order to overcome the problems and as a consequence points in the direction of specific therapeutic interventions.

Table 3.6 shows how it looks for Annabelle.

Table 3.6

Problem	Type of Problem	Intervention
Fatigue	Physiological Excess	Behavioural Activation
Irritability	Emotional Excess	Cognitive Restructuring, Behavioural Activation
Screaming and shouting	Behavioural Excess	Cognitive Restructuring, communication skills and problems solving skills
Perfectionism	Cognitive Excess	Cognitive Restructuring
		Behavioural Experiments

Assessment: feeding back information

When the therapist has completed the assessment, this needs to be shared with the client. An assessment takes as long as it needs to take. However, in general it needs to be remembered that the formulation is a *hypothesis*, which will be tested by the therapy. If the therapy is successful then the formulation was correct. If on the other hand the therapy does not produce the required results then the formulation needs to be revisited. In general most therapists take between two and five sessions to complete an assessment. The exact number of sessions needed depends on the complexity of the pathology.

Sharing the results of the assessment and the formulation with the client is a strategy that helps clients to become their own best therapist. Sharing the formulation with the client (in a neutral, low-key fashion) is the first test of the formulation. If it cannot be explained to the client, if the formulation does not 'stand up' to the client's feedback then it perhaps needs some more work. Through this clients get a better understanding of their situation. It is, however, of the utmost importance that all the information is provided in a neutral way and that the *client* draw conclusions from this. The task of the therapist is to coach clients in the decision-making process. The therapist is not the one who should prove that clients have problems or that change is necessary. The therapist always leaves responsibility with the client to draw conclusions from the facts.

Based on the situation of the client and the expert knowledge of the therapist a decision can be reached on whether the problem is real or imagined; whether change is needed or not.

Table 3.7 is an excerpt of the second part of the informing phase with our client Annabelle.

Table 3.7

Interview	Comments
Therapist: We are now at the stage whereby I would be able to present to you the findings of the assessment. Is that still ok with you?	
Annabelle: Sounds scary, as if you are going to analyse what is wrong with me.	
Therapist: Sounds scary … and yes there is an element to this whereby I put everything you told me together and come up with ideas where the issues are that cause problems and what you can do about it, if you would want to. Let me know if it gets too scary.	
Annabelle: OK, let's hear it then!	
Therapist: First of all you told me that there are a number of aspects of your life that you really don't like: you feel tired most of the time (we monitored this and there was during the week we recorded your energy levels not one part of the day that you felt energetic); most days your mood is pretty low and small things that happen can make you completely lose your temper with your husband and children (this happens two or thee times a week) and the screaming and shouting on your part can go on for hours until you are completely exhausted. These are all things you find unpleasant in your life and from the way you talked about it, you are a bit ashamed of the screaming.	Summarising the areas in client's life she has expressed dissatisfaction with.
Annabelle: Yes, especially screaming at John and the children, how can I do that? I am such a bad mother.	
Therapist: If I can just stop you there. I don't want you to accuse yourself of having these problems. The way you talk about them seemed to indicate that you really would like to change these things: be more energetic, feel more upbeat and when confronted with problems; problem solve and discuss with the children and John. Did I get that right?	Therapist interrupts.
Annabelle: Absolutely, I really want and need to get rid of this tiredness and this gloomy mood. And also my histrionic outbursts need to stop.	
Therapist: You really want to make a change!	
Annabelle: Definitely!	
Therapist: I also asked you questions and you completed some forms and questionnaires to help us	

Table 3.7 *(Continued)*

Interview	Comments
understand what the driving forces are behind these problem feelings and problem behaviours. Is it ok if I talk a bit about this now?	
Annabelle: And now you are going to tell me what a bad person I am!	
Therapist: Well if you call someone who wants to do things to perfection, who has very high standards for herself and who is inclined to sacrifice her needs in favour of other people's needs bad, then you are right!	Providing information about the attitudes and beliefs that contribute to the problem.
Annabelle: So you haven't found that I am an evil, bad and lazy person?	
Therapist: Far from it. The three things that I mentioned: wanting to do things to perfection; having very high standards for your own behaviour and trying to please other people, are these traits you recognise in yourself?	Repetition, ensuring client hears the message and checking for agreement.

Collaboration and Negotiating Phase

A third phase consists of the collaboration negotiation between therapist and client. By the end of the information phase a client should have made a decision: do I want to continue this way or do I want to change?

It is important that the therapist doesn't have strong and outspoken opinions on whether and how the client should change. The client has to decide whether change is needed and how the change is going to be achieved. These are all the client's decisions, but the therapist needs to provide objective information about the client's situation and the change/therapy options so the client can make an informed choice.

The client can then choose a treatment goal and method, based on the information the therapist has provided.

Returning to the interviews with Annabelle, Table 3.8 shows what happens. In this extract the therapist presents rudimentary links between the client's way of doing life and the problems the client experiences. This is extremely important as it assists the client in understanding the reasons behind certain interventions.

Reflection on assessment and formulation

In this chapter we have outlined the detailed and meticulous process of assessment and formulation. To do this 'our way' is needed because we propose idiosyncratic treatment plans. It is therefore essential to identify why the clients 'need' the problem behaviours. The therapist needs to go on an information gathering quest but in doing so needs to keep the client on side.

Table 3.8

Interview	Comments
Therapist: From what you have told me, there seems to be a direct link between your perfectionism, high standards and your incredible hard work. Your high standards also stand in the way of taking time out for yourself or to have 'me' time. Having no 'me' time and rarely achieving what you want to achieve is a certain recipe for feeling down and glum.	Summarising information the client has presented before and summarising the links between various elements.
Annabelle: So you are saying that my drive to do things well, to perfection and not giving myself any free time leads to depression and feeling miserable?	Client asks a clarifying question.
Therapist: Psychological research certainly has demonstrated that and if we look at your situation that certainly seems to be the case. Now these high standards and this perfectionism is something you learned from a young age. Your mother constantly imprinted on your mind the importance of perfection, her mission statement as you remembered was: Average is never good enough! As you recall it, your mum's intention was not to make you miserable. She truly believed that salvation lies in unrelenting hard work.	Therapist takes it away from his own opinion, but links it with research, to avoid an argument with client.
Annabelle: Yes, when I was young and was sitting down reading a book or a magazine or just resting, she always used to say: 'No rest for the wicked, let me give you something to do', and she herself was always busy. She could make such a drama when things were not just right!	Client provides further historical data confirming the picture.
Therapist: We also discovered that when you are in a gloomy mood or when you notice that things have not gone the way you want it, that you don't seem to have ways to discuss this with others (apart from screaming and shouting). And the only way you talk to yourself is also very punitive and critical. So we have as 'pushers' for the problems: high unrelenting standards leading to too much hard work and too little 'Annabelle' time and not having the communication skills to discuss moments of upset with others (or in a kind way with yourself). Any thoughts about that?	Further summary.
Annabelle: Well, that's just the way I am. I don't think I could change any of that.	Client makes what sounds like an 'unmotivated' statement, but often when people say: 'That is the way I am, I don't think I can change.' The hidden meaning behind that is that the person would like to change but lack 'self-efficacy'.

(Continued)

Table 3.8 *(Continued)*

Interview	Comments
Therapist: If I understood you right, you really would like to change the screaming and shouting, you would like to be more energetic and more upbeat. Based on our discussion you would have to work on your perfectionism, work less hard, include more 'Annabelle' time in your life and learn to communicate differently. What you are saying is that you think it would be completely impossible to do that.	Motivational interviewing: overshooting: getting the client to doubt her earlier 'I can't'.
Annabelle: No, not impossible, but it sounds quite daunting.	Success!
Therapist: So working on letting go your perfectionism, learning new ways of communicating, working less and playing more sounds daunting but is something you would like to go ahead with.	
Annabelle: Yes, as you say these are the pushers of my unhappiness.	

We introduced a chronological sequence of starting CBT with personality disorders: from eliciting, via informing to negotiation and collaboration. The BASIC-ID and SORCC models were introduced as helpful tools to use in putting together formulations.

Understanding check

Things you should be able to do after reading this chapter:

1. Describe the six 'Ws'.
2. Describe the chronological steps at the beginning of CBT.
3. Explain the differences between formulation, functional analysis and topographical analysis.
4. Explain the acronyms SORCC and BASIC-ID.
5. Explain why information feeding back from therapist to client is just as important as data collection during assessment.

4

SOCIALISING THE CLIENT TO CBT, IDENTIFYING PROBLEMS AND GOALS, AND TREATMENT EVALUATION

In the previous chapter we focused on how the therapist can gradually gain an understanding of source and maintenance of clients' problems. This process of investigation needs to be combined and complemented by two other elements of CBT in these beginning stages of therapy: socialising the client to CBT and identifying problems and goals.

Socialising to the CBT Model

The client needs to become a gifted amateur in CBT. It is essential therefore that the client learns that:

- Problems are the result of an often long learning process.
- Problems are influenced by unhelpful/irrational thinking.
- The brain sometimes learns to have a mind of its own.

What do clients need to learn about CBT? It is our belief that the task of the therapist is to elevate the client's knowledge about CBT to the level of a gifted amateur. Clients need to understand that: problems are the end product of a learning process; thinking influences what we do and feel in a major way and we have developed beliefs about ourselves, others and the future that can be unhelpful and need changing.

Socialising the client to the CBT model does not occur at a specific moment during therapy. It is an ongoing process whereby the therapist provides brief explanations but mainly utilises clients' presentation of their problems as opportunities to highlight the workings of the CBT model. Socialising to the CBT model is therefore an integral part of the assessment and treatment process.

Problems are the result of a learning process

It is helpful for clients to understand that their current predicament is the result of a learning and adaptation process. Depression and avoidance did not suddenly appear yesterday, excessive drinking did not suddenly start on a specific date. More often than not a long learning process preceded the emergence of the problem. Human beings are like creative learning machines. When we are confronted with situations that we find difficult, we try and find a way to deal with this. Many psychological problems are the result of this. A beloved family member dies, which results in natural grief and in order to cope with the pain the person develops feelings of extreme sadness and depression (and will report feeling numb, e.g. not feeling the grief any more). To feel alive again they develop a gambling habit. It is important for the therapist to realise that clients do not go out of their way to deliberately engage in this kind of learning: 'Oh, gee, I am grieving, that is a bit painful so let's get depressed, which after a while really sucks so let's liven things up and go to the casino …' This learning develops in a trial and error manner. People use their existing skills: they learn from models in their environment and informational feedback from their environment.

Problems are influenced by irrational thinking

Clients need to understand that what they say to themselves plays an enormous role in how they will feel. Clients need to be weaned off the idea that it is what happens to us that makes us feel our feelings. It will be important to teach clients that the meaning we give to what happens to us dictates how we will feel in any given situation. Clients need to learn that because they are human, they are very much prone to irrational thinking (e.g. the therapist needs to take away the implicit belief that only stupid people think irrationally). It is very easy to get into a mode of just paying lip-service to this concept in therapy. Clinicians should learn not to go along with clients that there are certain beliefs that are really true ('You have to be respectful, life should be fair, I should not make mistakes, other people should approve of me', etc.) If the client does not buy into this model, then cognitive restructuring interventions later on will be difficult.

We teach clients that their thinking develops along various lines. First, there is the automatic thinking: thoughts and images that pop into our mind without effort. Everyone has negative automatic thoughts (NATs) and will continue to have them. Whether we have problems as a result of these negative automatic thoughts depends on how much attention we give them. Just imagine what would happen if the depressed person would react to his or her negative automatic thoughts (life is hopeless, I am hopeless, my future is dark and grim) by simply ignoring them and get on with life and focus on his or her goal-directed deliberate thinking. In all likelihood the depression would be a lot less because it is the deliberate engagement with the NATS that causes trouble. The first burst of NATS might result in a sense of depression and sadness, but that will lift sooner rather than later if the person does not engage with these thoughts. So using deliberate thinking to engage with the NATS can be along rational lines (this is just a thought – no need to give it too much attention) or along an irrational path (oh my god, there I go again, can't get rid of this depression, I will not be able to cope with the day). This deliberate thinking is strongly influenced by the beliefs the client holds on to as well as his/her core beliefs and rules for living.

Beliefs are ideas about how the person, life and other people should be. Examples of beliefs are:

- If I don't score 100 per cent on this test I am such a loser.
- Life shouldn't be as difficult as it is.
- If I ask for help people will simply take advantage of me.

Core beliefs have a more absolute character to them (some authors would call them schemas):

- I have to be perfect.
- I am bad.
- Other people are out to do me harm.
- The world is a cesspit of misery.

A good metaphor to use with clients is to compare the whole thinking process with the workings of a computer. The NATS are the images you see on a computer screen. The beliefs can be compared with the software, while the core beliefs are like the hardware. The use of the keyboard can be seen as the deliberate thinking. If one reacts to the wrong message on the screen all might go wrong.

The brain has a mind of its own

Clients have to learn that they sometimes are the 'victim' of automatic processes in the brain. The emotional processing centre of the brain may send out an all-points alarm bulletin, before the thinking part of the brain has had a chance to look it over.

This plays a role in personality problems as well as in post-traumatic stress disorder and panic disorder. Clients with problems such as this frequently report noticing their body being in a full state of arousal, followed by their catastrophic thinking. Therapists may have a hard time identifying thoughts that triggered the physiological arousal, because there may have been none. The emotional regulation centre of the brain has, with a mind of its own, decided to signal to the body that danger is approaching. This signalling occurs much faster than the processing of the cortex. Consequently, the person experiences physical signs of anxiety without really knowing why. The post-hoc meaning-giving process (my heart is racing, I must be getting a heart attack) subsequently leads to anxiety, which further activates the arousal system.

How do we teach the client about the CBT model?

In our work we envisage four steps in teaching clients about the CBT model of working: explanation, factual demonstration, insightful demonstration and application.

It cannot be emphasised too much that this explanation should be tailored to the needs of the client. For a client who impresses the therapist being psychologically minded the explanation will have to be different compared with a client who finds it difficult to grasp that thinking and feeling play a role in doing! In other words the therapist has to 'assess' the client with respect to his/her need regarding a CBT explanation. Sometimes we need to supply clients with a detailed and sophisticated explanation of how thinking facilitates feelings and how feelings influence behaviours; followed by explaining how our thinking goes into an irrational overdrive. At other times we just need to explain that problems emerge because we have learned to react in an unhelpful manner and we need to train ourselves to react in more helpful ways.

Explanation

The explanation step is often done in the first session, whereby the therapist briefly outlines the core characteristics of CBT and the underpinning issues. This can often be done with a brief introduction, after an initial overview of the client's problems is established.

Here are some helpful sentences we have been using over the years:

'Well it is perhaps a good moment for me to briefly outline what kind of therapy I do. I work as a cognitive behaviour therapist. What do you know about this form of therapy?'

'You are very right, cognitive behaviour therapy, or CBT for short, sees it as very important that people change their behaviour. For instance, if you are terrified of meeting people, then it is not good enough to just become less afraid, if the person still avoids meeting people. In short, and we will talk more about that when we will look in more detail at the issues you struggle with, CBT believes that most problems are learned and can be unlearned, it believes that our thinking plays an important role in the development and maintenance of unhelpful feelings and behaviours. For example, if I believe that other people will always be nasty to me, I will be more inclined to feel anxious in situations with them and avoid people. Can you think of

(Continued)

---

an example of your own life where what you were thinking influenced what you were feeling and doing?'

'OK, a few more things about how we work in these sessions. CBT is a pretty structured form of therapy; we start by making a list of things to talk about, we prioritise the items on that list and often there are tasks that I will ask you to do between sessions. In other words, for CBT to work for you, you will have to work CBT. How does that sound?'

This first explanation is intended to set the scene, but also to inform the client that there is no such thing as a free lunch. Especially with clients whose problems are long-standing and deeply ingrained in their way of being (as personality difficulties are) or clients with a long history of mental health interventions in a medical setting (again, as people with personality difficulties are) this is often a difficult moment. They often see therapy as something that is done to them, not something that they will do to themselves. We often use the phrase: 'Using CBT will teach you to become your own best therapist.' The therapist needs to take careful note of clients' responses to the explanation and be very aware that some clients want to do therapy in a passive mode. These clients may be looking for a therapist who fixes their problems and the first task in therapy (pre-therapy) may be to get the client ready for CBT.

Factual demonstration

The aim here is to help the client understand the links between stimuli (events that happen), thoughts, feelings, behaviours and sensations. Clients need to 'understand' the links between these elements. We do not mean scientific understanding, but the client needs to 'know' that there are influential links between the various components. An example of this is:

When something goes wrong, I immediately think the worst has happened and perceive this as a terrible catastrophe. Because I want to avoid this I work very hard and do not give myself any rest. This makes me very tired most of the time and prone to making mistakes.

During this step, there is no talk by the therapist about irrational thinking or maladaptive behaviours, as the main aim is for the client to understand connections. A special difficulty arises with clients who have long-standing problems. They will have developed a 'blind spot' for the connections between certain elements. Clients may not see that there is a connection between what they do and how they feel. (For instance, Lisette was staying in her room with the curtains closed all the time, playing very sad music and eating lots of junk food. As a consequence she feels very depressed and self-harms, but she does not see that her behaviour influences her mood; she perceives her depressed mood as a given that 'makes' her stay in her room and listen to sad music.)

This step, using clients' personal experiences to illustrate the idea of connectedness between mood, thinking and behaving can take quite a few sessions with some clients. Therapist and client may need to review quite a few examples from the client's life before it 'clicks' for the client. Patience is a virtue, while good Socratic dialogue and motivational interviewing should be the style of the conversation.

Insightful demonstration

The aim of this step is to help clients understand that their thinking is irrational and that the problem behaviours are self-defeating and maladaptive. In order to achieve this, client and therapist need to revisit explicitly the CBT model and to review examples from the client illustrating high levels of unhealthy negative feelings or maladaptive behaviour. The therapist may need to do some teaching on rational and irrational thinking. This step adds to the previous step the notion that the thinking that influences the negative feeling and/or promotes problem behaviours is not based on facts and is irrational.

Clients often find this a challenging step. Most people think that they are rational and sensible. It is important to remain 'Socratic' and motivational here and not go into a didactic style. Sometimes clients really can't see their thinking as unhelpful or irrational and then we may have to find other ways of 'labelling' it in order to make further investigation into thinking acceptable. Lisette, for example, had as a core thought: 'I should get what I want, if not that is absolutely terrible, and if I don't get what I want I need to show them how much it upsets me!' For her this was in this phase of her treatment a law of the universe. By inviting her to think about this mission statement for her life from a purely pragmatic way ('Does holding on to this mission statement get you from life what you want?') it became possible to get her to accept that her original ('I should get what I want, if not that is absolutely terrible, and if I don't get what I want I need to show them how much it upsets me!') might be a law of the universe, but it did not work to her advantage and it might be an idea to investigate how she could get more out of life.

Application

The previous three steps need to be completed before the therapist embarks on change-directed interventions. This step can often only be taken when the client is completely convinced that the CBT model will work for them. The aim is for the client to be able to apply the CBT model to their own problems and have the ability to explain how their unhelpful thinking results in negative feelings and the promotion of self-defeating behaviours. Most clients with personality difficulties will need to experience significant change before they will be able to really apply the model to themselves.

And what is therapy CBT-style all about?

The therapist also needs to prepare the client for the style and structure of CBT. The client needs to appreciate a form of psychological therapy that has the characteristics as described in Chapter 2.

Fine-tuning Problems and Goals

Based on the shared formulation client and therapist review the initial problems and goals and decide on fine-tuning and prioritising these. Now is the time to really define the goals into specific and concrete terms. Here is a list of questions that the therapist can ask and that will assist the client to define the goals more specifically:

- What would you do more of/less of if your problem no longer bothered you?
- What would have changed in your life if the problem was no more?
- What are you not doing now as a result of your problems?

It is important to define goals that are as specific as possible, and they should be within clients' control. So a problem should not be defined as 'losing weight' but 'going to the gym three times a week'; not 'getting rid of my depression' but 'getting up each day and going for a brisk walk for 30 minutes'.

In this stage of therapy, client and therapist are left with a list of problems (things that are currently happening that bother the client) and goals (things the client would like to happen but cannot put into effect). The therapist has come up with a hypothesis (the formulation) for how this discrepancy between the current situation and the client's ambition came to be. Based on the formulation and the redefined problems and goals, a detailed therapy plan is now discussed with the client.

Criteria for Goal Selection

The client decides upon which problems and goals therapy should focus, but the therapist can provide guidance. Although it is impossible to develop a list of criteria that would be appropriate for each case, some general rules can be stated that help clinicians to take into account technical and professional realities as well as basic theory in selecting possible therapy targets. The following list presents a few of the items to be considered (Gambrill, 1977).

- What are the negative consequences of the problem?
- What is the likelihood that the target behaviour is amenable to change with the available methods and within the limits of the clinician's competence, the resources of the client, and the tolerance of the social environment?
- To what extent and in what way would the client's present life improve if the treatment goal were attained?
- Are there any negative side effects of selecting this target for the client or others?
- Is the proposed change in the target behaviour or situation consistent with the client's goals and values?
- To what extent is the client motivated toward attainment of this goal in relation to other goals?
- Will the goal be maintained by the client or the natural environment for long post-therapy effectiveness?

Prioritising Interventions: moving from *outside* → *in*

In prioritising what to start working on first there are two types of guidelines. The first guideline is set out in the points discussed previously. A problem issue that threatens the life of client or others will need to be prioritised. A second guideline is the centrality of the problem. Intuitively most clinicians would want to start the therapy process with problems that are central to the formulation, e.g. problems that are considered to be at the cause of other problems. We would counsel against that. It is much better to work from the 'outside inwards'. This in a way feels counter-intuitive: let's get rid of the cause of the problem and all will be well. The metaphor of a high-rise building may be helpful. Let's assume you have to demolish a 20-storey building and you need to do it by hand, without making it crash on nearby buildings. Which floors would be easiest to demolish: the ground-floor, floor 20 or the foundation? If one could destroy the foundations the whole thing would come crashing down, but that may have some collateral damage. Best to start at the top and carefully bring all the demolition rubbish down. The same goes for psychological problems. Peripheral problems are often easier dealt with then more central problems (and consequently giving the client a bigger sense of competence and success). It is also a gradual way of taking the underpinning problems of the central problem away.

Treatment Evaluation

Evaluation of treatment is an essential part of CBT. To ensure evaluation is done properly, it is important to start the treatment in a way that makes evaluation possible. There are various ways to do this. The therapist can use a set of measures at the start of treatment and give them to the client again at treatment completion. A more personalised way to evaluate treatment is to focus on the problems and goals the client identified.

Therapist and client can complete the 'problem and goals form' shown in Table 4.1 at beginning and treatment end.

Table 4.1

Treatment Evaluation Form			
Evaluation: ( ) Beginning ( ) Session nr. ____ ( ) End of treatment			
Problems	How severe do you rate this problem? 0 = not a problem 10 = extremely severe	How much does this problem interfere with your daily functioning? 0 = not at all 10 = it makes life impossible	What would you like to achieve with respect to this problem? (and list as goals)
1.			
2.			
3.			
4.			
5.			
Goals	How far are you away from achieving this goal? 0 = goal achieved 10 = could not be further away from the goal		
1.			
2.			
3.			
4.			
5.			

It is very important not to postpone evaluation of treatment to the last session, but to make it an ongoing part of CBT. In general to 'take stock' and to check how the therapy is moving the client in the right direction, an evaluation moment every six to eight sessions would be a good idea.

Having regular evaluation moments during therapy is also an implicit preparation for the final moment when therapy comes to an end. This prepares the client for the final goodbye and provides an opportunity for the client to bring up any problems they predict in the future. It also is a moment where the therapist can check with the client how she/he feels about ending therapy.

Severity rating before treatment

The client indicates how severe they perceive the problem is at the beginning of treatment and they indicate how severe they now think their problem is. This takes into account the client's incorrect (exaggerated or minimising) perception of their problems at the beginning of treatment. For instance, a problem drinker may evaluate his drinking problem as 5 at the beginning of treatment, but looking back might increase this to 9. A person with a worry problem might evaluate this as 10 at the beginning, but looking back might think that 6 would be a better rating.

Interference rating with daily life before treatment

Here the client rates how much the problem interferes with daily life and again the client is asked to do two ratings. One was done at the beginning of treatment and one is done now looking back.

Severity rating post-treatment and interference rating with daily life post-treatment

Here the client gives a rating of how he/she perceives the severity of this problem at the end of treatment. It becomes immediately clear why we had the client re-evaluate the severity of the problem at beginning of treatment. The problem drinker who rated his drinking as a 5 would not have made progress if he rated his problem at the end of treatment also with a 5. But by getting him to re-evaluate the problem with the benefit of hindsight and insight we get a more realistic evaluation.

Goals set with respect to this problem

Client and therapist revisit the goals that were set regarding this problem and include goals that were added during the course of treatment.

Ending Therapy

In our experience a very matter of fact approach to ending therapy works best. The ongoing and regular evaluations alert clients during therapy of the finite character of this relationship. Despite this, clients whose problem presentation includes strong dependence on others and a fear of abandonment may display difficulties when the issue of ending therapy comes up. The end of therapy is perceived by these clients as something to be feared and as a learned response they will display habitual behaviours to avert this anxiety-provoking event. These habitual behaviours are the self-defeating behaviours that have been the focus of therapy.

When the client's fears regarding ending therapy flare up *before the client has acquired the skills to deal with this*, then the therapist has two tasks:

- Take the lead in calming the client down (not by reassurance, but by providing factual information).
- Identify the skill the client needs to learn in order to deal with future eruptions of this fear and prioritise this in the treatment plan.

When the client's fears regarding ending therapy flare up *after the client has acquired the skills to deal with this*, then the therapist has one task: to invite the client to identify the skills she/he needs to deploy to overcome this obstacle and guide the client through this process.

Reassurance by telling the client that therapy will last as long as it takes to get the client better, that the therapist will always be there, and any other form of unrealistic promise should be avoided at all costs.

Factual information, i.e. telling the client that the prospect of being without therapy is indeed scary, but it is the beginning of therapy and there are many more skills to be learned that will enable the client to deal with difficulties in the future, is needed.

In the end stages of therapy it becomes a pitfall to rescue the client. Here the client will be asked to apply skills learned in therapy to their personal distress and the role of the therapist has changed from a leader/instructor to a coach.

For clients who find ending extremely difficult, we have used a structured from of gradual reducing the intensity of therapy helpful. From weekly session to fortnightly face-to-face sessions and one telephone contact in between, from there to just fortnightly sessions and so on. What we also incorporated in this were a number of 'extra' phone and face-to-face appointments that could be made outside the structure. For instance, with one client we planned the end of therapy over a period of six months. Over this period the client had four extra face-to-face sessions and two phone sessions that she could schedule when she needed them – the structure is shown in Table 4.2.

Table 4.2

Month	Face-to-face (1 hour)	Phone (30 minutes)
1	2	2
2	1	3
3	1	3
4	1	2
5	1	1
6	1	

Contemplation on socialising to CBT, problems and goals, and therapy evaluation

This chapter has dealt with three important cornerstones of what makes CBT a different psychological therapy from many other forms of treatment. First of all there is the socialising to the CBT model. It is essential that clients learn to understand his/her problems from a CBT perspective. The goal of CBT is that clients acquire skills that enable them to continue to overcome problems after therapy has completed. This means that CBT is a therapy that needs to go beyond 'doing things to clients': clients need to learn how to deal with their problems on their own. Becoming you own best therapist could be the mission statement of any CBT.

The second cornerstone is the identification of specific problems and goals. We often conceptualise CBT as a journey. The process is similar: you have to know where you are before you can decide on the route to where you want to go. Identifying specific problems also has a motivation enhancing effect as the client can clearly see which personal suffering or discomfort will be alleviated through therapy. Goal setting is very important to offer guidance to client and therapist in respect to where the therapeutic interventions need to take the client.

Evaluation and ending are two important components of any psychological therapy. In CBT, however, treatment evaluation is an ongoing process. In the beginning of therapy information about the problems and problem severity is collected in such a manner that it makes evaluations possible. In CBT regular treatment evaluations during treatment are done, in longer treatments every six–eight sessions. Conducting regular treatment evaluations is good practice to keep therapist and client on track to work towards agreed goals. The added benefit is that it is an ongoing reminder of the process of therapy: having a beginning and an ending.

Understanding check

Things you should be able to do after reading this chapter:

1 Describe important issues regarding fine-tuning problems and goals.
2 List criteria for a good problem and goal definition.
3 Know what needs to be worked on first: deeper underlying issues or more superficial symptoms.
4 Understand why it is important to explain CBT to the client.
5 Explain CBT to clients.
6 Explain why it is necessary to explain CBT to clients.
7 Explain the steps a therapist needs to take to explain the CBT model to clients.
8 Use problem severity measures to evaluate therapy.

5

STRUCTURING SESSIONS: FROM AGENDA
SETTING TO HOMEWORK

In this chapter you will learn about:

- The importance of structuring sessions.
- The importance of agenda setting.
- Ongoing session evaluation.

CBT is structured in its overall process and in the organisation of individual sessions.

After an agenda has been set and the homework from the previous session is reviewed, the therapist and the client proceed to discuss the other issues on the agenda in order of importance. Generally, it is possible to make progress on one to three problem areas in a particular session.

In addressing a typical issue, the therapist usually begins by asking the client a series of questions in order to clarify the nature of the difficulty. For example, is the client misinterpreting events? To what extent is the problem 'real'? Are the client's expectations realistic? Are there alternative explanations or solutions? If the problem is symptomatic or behavioural (e.g. insomnia, appetite disturbance, low mood, or 'overwhelming' chores or tasks), more specific history taking and behavioural analysis may be necessary. At the end of this questioning process, the therapist suggests focusing on one or two key thoughts, assumptions, images, or behaviours during the session. Once such targets are selected, the therapist recommends a cognitive or behavioural intervention and explains the rationale for use of the technique to the client. These procedures may include actions such as setting up an experiment, role playing or cognitive rehearsal, generating alternatives, weighing advantages and disadvantages, and activity scheduling (Beck et al., 1979).

Toward the end of the session, the therapist again asks the client for feedback. It is generally useful to encourage questions about potential areas of confusion and to ask the client to summarise the major points of the session. Finally, the therapist suggests a relevant homework assignment. The homework is tailored to help the client apply what is being learned in CBT during the interval between sessions.

Although the structure of the CBT session illustrated above does not change substantially as treatment progresses, the content does. The initial sessions are generally concerned with setting priorities, building empathy and rapport, reducing hopelessness, demonstrating the relationship between thoughts and feelings, identifying errors in thinking and making rapid progress on readily solvable problems.

Session structure during assessment

Using an empathic and businesslike style, therapists aim to stick to a programme like this with clients who present with an average suitability for CBT. Clients with very serious communication problems or serious interpersonal issues (personality disorders) may cause the therapist to deviate from this. It is, however, very important to highlight deviations and not do it 'quietly'. Make deviations explicit and identify the reasoning behind the deviation. Our suggestion, however, is *never* skip the setting of the agenda, reviewing homework, giving homework and evaluation of the session.

Setting the agenda

Agenda setting is a crucial element of each session. In a first session it is perhaps better to start by saying something like: 'You have made an appointment to see me. I am sure we have lots of things to discuss. Let's make a list of the things we want to talk about in this first session. What are issues you would like to talk about today?' And after client gives a few topics: 'Now what I would like to discuss are the following points. Are there any more things you would like to raise in this session?'

Explain the process

In a first session it is important to explain that the therapist is first going to do an assessment, which will last a couple of sessions. At completion the therapist will present the client with an overview of the results. Based on these a treatment plan will be set up. The client's views on issues will be welcomed and together client and therapist will establish an intervention plan that suits the client.

Ascertain presenting symptoms and complaints

Now it is time to ask the client what it is that he/she has come to see a therapist about. The previous steps need not take longer than about five minutes. The therapist should keep in mind that an empathic but businesslike style of discussion and inquiry is the optimal approach. Too often, beginning and not-so beginning therapists fritter time away by talking about non-relevant issues in the name of rapport building. It is our view that time is valuable and needs to be used in a focused way.

In this section the therapist wants to know which symptoms the client is concerned about. It is important to get to the bottom of things and get a comprehensive overview.

Inquire regarding all of the complaints

Establish whether you have heard all clients' concerns. 'Is there anything else?' brings sometimes surprising results! At this point the therapist just lists the concerns. When the list is fairly complete, it is perhaps time to summarise and categorise the issues.

An example of a list of concerns: sleep badly, can't get out of bed in the morning, stopped enjoying things, feel miserable, don't like eating anymore and can't concentrate.

From complaints to problems: the provisional problem list

Complaints are the things that the client mentions that are bothering him or her. Translating complaints into a problem list means that we have to look beyond the presentation and ask ourselves, and the client, what is the problem with having this symptom? Problems need to be defined very specifically and focused on changeable entities.

Deciding what is a 'good problem' and what is a 'bad problem' can be done by revisiting the guidelines in the previous chapter. In summary: good problems are issues the client has potential control over and bad problems are outside the client's direct control. For instance, the client has no control over how fair or unfair other people are.

Good problems:

- I don't do anything enjoyable because I am depressed.
- I feel depressed and don't have fun with my family anymore.
- My partner and I have frequent arguments and then I become too angry.
- I can't speak up for myself because I am too shy.

Bad problems:

- Life sucks.
- People are so unfair.
- My parents abused me.

Provisional goals list

Based on the provisional problems list, client and therapist now create a list of goals. The therapist asks the client to state what he/she wants to achieve for each identified problem. Questions that will assist clients to be specific and concrete are:

- How would your life be different if you would achieve that goal?
- What would be different in your life after having achieved that goal?
- How would I be able to see that you had achieved your goal?

First socialisation to the CBT model
Once the goals have been established the therapist moves into explaining CBT.

Application of CBT to symptoms and problems
At this point it is important to apply your explanation to the problems and goals of the client. Your job is now to use the 'theory' you have provided the client with to explain the practical problems and/or goals the client presents you with. In other words you explain how learning about thinking and changing thinking might be beneficial or how learning skills may be beneficial.

Understanding check
This should become a standard element in the repertoire of each CBT therapist. Once a concept is explained to the client, check whether the client has understood it. The best way to do this is to ask the client to explain it back to you, as if he is explaining to a good friend what he has learned today.

Homework discussion
Homework is an important feature of CBT. The homework assignments at completion of the first session can be: monitoring the frequency, intensity and duration of the problem(s), completing standard questionnaires and perhaps some reading about a CBT perspective on the client's symptoms. Remember to give homework that will assist in the assessment. Completed homework in this phase should be helpful in completing the conceptualisation.

Evaluation
Take time at completion of each session to check how the client has experienced the session. Topics to check for are: Did I do things you did not like and what were they? Did I do things that were helpful and what were they? What did you learn today? Any tips for the next session?

A more structured way of getting feedback is to use the form shown in Tables 5.1 and 5.2.

Therapist works

The therapist cannot be idle between sessions. As soon as possible after the session it is important to evaluate what has been said in the session. How do the symptoms fit together? What kind of hypothesis regarding formulation can be formulated? What is the plan for the next sessions? In CBT doing therapy is a process whereby the therapist constantly tries to give meaning and understanding to the presentation of the client. Why does the client have these problems? How did they emerge and how are they currently maintained?

Table 5.1

Better insight into and understanding of my problems.

Methods or techniques for better dealing with my problems.

Techniques in defining and solving my everyday problems.

Greater ability to express what was troubling me.

Increase confidence in myself.

Greater ability to cope with negative feelings such as anger, depression, guilt and anxiety.

Better control over what I do and don't do.

Greater ability to recognise my unhelpful thinking.

Greater ability to correct my unhelpful thinking.

Better ways of having a balanced life.

Increased motivation to do something about my problem.

Table 5.2

I could trust my therapist

The things my therapist said or suggested seemed helpful.

The therapist seemed to know what he/she was doing.

The therapist did not seem to care about what happens to me.

The therapist often did not seem to understand me.

The therapist acted condescending or talked down to me.

The therapist was too quiet and passive.

My therapist is too bossy.

My therapist talks too much.

The therapist misses the point.

My therapist did not give me enough chance to express myself.

The therapist is a good listener.

The therapist makes me really think about my problems.

The therapist teaches me valuable skills.

Session structure during the intervention phase of treatment

Once the client and therapist have discussed the implications of the assessment a treatment programme can be started. Session structure does not change much, but the content is now increasingly about therapeutic interventions that are tried out or practised in the sessions, after which the client will try them out between sessions. The discussion of homework is filled with client reporting back on their success and/or difficulties regarding these therapeutic tasks.

Agenda setting remains important. The temptation may be to skip it ('We – client and therapist – know what we want to talk about, so let's save time and just start'). This assumption has resulted in trouble for many therapists.

A common mistake of beginning therapists is to assume that clients will be able to apply the CBT model after the few explanations they have received. Good CBT means that the therapist uses every opportunity to highlight and explain the CBT model, using examples from what the client brings to therapy.

During agenda setting, clients will often mention issues and problems that they have encountered in the previous period. A good collaborative way to review these problem issues is to discuss them while using the SORCC format (topographical analysis). In doing so the therapist and client will rapidly find out what kind of *problem* in CBT terms we are dealing with and which *interventions* may be useful. In this phase of treatment, problem situations are not merely reviewed, they are now linked with specific CBT interventions intended to bring about change.

EXAMPLE

Mrs Robinson is a 43-year-old accountant. Her main problem was depression and aggressive outbursts (a psychiatrist has given her a diagnosis of borderline personality disorder). Now in her fifth session she wants to put on the agenda 'Feeling angry and becoming aggressive for no reason whatsoever'. The therapist invites her to mention a situation during last week when she was feeling angry and, as she describes it, for no reason. Mrs Robinson comes up with Thursday afternoon, just before leaving work to go home. She describes how suddenly she felt this unreasonably strong surge of anger towards her fellow workers in the office. Table 5.3 shows how a SORCC analysis would look.

Table 5.3

Situation	Organism Internal Events	Responses Overt Behaviour	Consequences	Contingency
Time: end of working day Place: at work People: alone, others have gone home (1½ hr before) Behaviour: going through expense forms, incorrectly completed.	Sensations: tense Thoughts: I have failed once again; why can't I just complete work on time like everyone else; no one ever helps me; they are all in it to make my life difficult Feeling: sudden rage towards all colleagues (combined with a thought: why can't they just let me get on with my work and followed by guilt).	Going home, but tasks are unfinished.	Cognitive: self-criticism for leaving work without finishing tasks Behavioural: taking work home, cancelling meeting with friends; acting aggressively towards family; lock self in bedroom with a bottle of gin Feeling: guilt towards friends, family and guilt towards colleagues; self-pity.	Overwork happens regularly, cancelling private engagements for work happens regularly, self-critical feedback occurs when not living up to self-imposed standard.

(Continued)

(Continued)

From this SORCC analysis we established that Mrs Robinson's late work was partly due to her colleagues asking her for help during the day (and consequently she could not do her own work) and her boss giving her too much work (she never said no and always finished tasks before a deadline, so he did not get feedback from her that it was too much). Mrs Robinson simply did not know how to say 'no' (skills training) and had developed irrational thinking strategies around saying 'no', not finishing work and giving priority to her private life (cognitive restructuring).

What we focused on in this session was how to express negative feelings as the therapist and Mrs Robinson found that to be an essential ingredient in triggering and maintaining this problem. Mrs Robinson identified two situations at work where she could have expressed negative feelings and asked her boss and colleagues to behave differently towards her (saying 'no' to extra work, informing others how their behaviour made her feel bad). The therapist suggested the home situation as a moment when negative feelings could have been expressed: informing her family about her state of inner turmoil and asking them to be kind to her and spoil her a bit. In the session we explained a structure of expressing negative feelings to Mrs Robinson and then practised it in several short role-plays.

Difficulties in session structure

Having a good structure for delivering effective CBT is all good and well, but what if the client does not want to be structured? Frequently we are confronted with cognitive behaviour therapists who get 'lost' in working with challenging clients. They come to us for clinical supervision and eagerly bring a recording of a session with the difficult client. The implicit expectancy is that we will be able to offer some unique insights regarding specific interventions that are needed with this client. Too often this is not the case and the problem is far simpler. The therapist has been 'seduced' by the client to let go of the structure of therapy. Clients with personality difficulties have often years of experience in imposing *their* structure on other people and this has led to their current predicament. Most people with personality difficulties will not deliberately attempt to derail the therapist and therapy (the exception may be people with a psychopathic personality). They just do what they always do and by using the session structure the therapist creates a first change: the client can no longer 'do what they do'. Here are a few examples of 'destructuring' strategies clients might use:

- 'Before we start, I just have to tell you this ...' Before you realise it you have spent most of the session listening to a client's story of which the relevance to therapy you don't yet know. The best response is: 'If I can just stop you there, sorry for interrupting – is this an issue you would like to put on the agenda for today?'

- The client does not stop talking and drifts from issue to issue in their chaotic ramblings. When this happens the therapist needs to go back to the agenda (oops, there was no agenda …). It may be necessary to bring the client back to the agenda over and over again. This could also be a signal that the agenda has been set rather unilaterally and that in future more collaboration is needed.
- Every session there seems to be a new major problem. In these situations it is important to review the formulation and 'place' these new problems in the formulation. It also may be necessary for the therapist to invest in some thinking time: perhaps the 'new' problems are not so new after all – is there a core issue in all these problems that links with the formulation?
- 'We don't need to do the session evaluation; you are the best therapist I ever had and that is not going to change. We can use the time more productively.' The strategy here is obvious: 'Thanks for that nice compliment, I agree we should not spend more time on the session evaluation than is needed. I really value a brief moment of reflection on the session at the end and would find it difficult to deliver the best therapy possible if we deviated from the plan.'

In general it is advisable not to let things drift, but to address 'destructuring' as soon as it erupts. Do not wait and hope that it will get better, as it won't; it is your job to assist the client to make optimal use of therapy and the structure of CBT is a key element.

Reflection on session structure

The structured format of CBT is very helpful in working with personality disorder. The stable predictability of this structure can become a helpful tool for clients. They know what to expect in each session and the collaboration between therapist and client is formally structured in the design of the sessions. The use of specific tools such as the SORCC model to discuss problem situations and to make it the stepping stone for the application of specific change directed interventions is very useful as clients can quickly learn how to present problem situations in a helpful way to the therapist.

Despite this, many therapists and clients don't like the structure. Therapists feel hemmed in and think they can't be spontaneous anymore. We would like to counter that by saying that driving a car can be great fun as long as everyone remembers on which side of the road to drive. Spontaneity and veering from the left to the right side of the road as one sees fit is dangerous and will lead to catastrophes. We have found that only clients who are really deeply attached to just being able to talk in an unstructured way don't like the session structure. Often these clients will say that, yes, they can see the structure is beneficial, but they feel so 'controlled' by it that they have to fight it. This does not have to result in problems as long as the client accepts the therapist's attempts to hold the structure.

Understanding check

Things you should be able to do after reading this chapter:

1 Describe the structure of a therapy session.
2 Explain the importance of sticking to the structure.
3 Outline the need for agenda setting.
4 Explain the usefulness of discussing specific problem occurrences using the SORCC format.
5 Review the importance of session evaluation, even when pressed for time.

6

INTERVENTIONS FOR (LASTING) CHANGE

In this chapter you will learn about:

- The mindset needed for working with clients having personality difficulties.
- The importance of treatment based on formulation.
- The SORCC model as a guiding light.
- Counter-therapeutic behaviours and how to deal with them.
- Impulse control problems and how to deal with them.
- The DTR as the cornerstone of CBT.
- Cognitive interventions.
- Behavioural interventions.
- Skills training interventions.

Spirit of CBT for people having personality difficulties

Colleagues often ask us: 'How can you work with such difficult/uncooperative clients? How can you work with clients who have done so many bad/evil things?' It is all a question of attitude. Working as a psychological therapist with clients who have personality difficulties makes it necessary to be very aware of one's own values, preferences and demands. It is necessary to realise that our values, preferences and demands will not necessarily be helpful ingredients in therapy if we allow them to play a role there. As psychological therapists working with clients having personality problems, we have to learn to 'accept what is' instead of 'demanding what should be'.

We have to learn to be very mindful of our own reactions to clients':

- counter-therapeutic behaviours in session (argumentative, criticising the therapist, threatening with self-harm/suicide)
- counter-therapeutic behaviours between sessions: not completing self-help tasks, self-harm, high-risk behaviours
- 'bad' behaviours between sessions that the client reports about during session: illegal acts, acts of violence.

As psychological therapists we have a specific role: applying evidence-based science to the client's problems so the client is able to lead a more fulfilling and less disruptive life. If the psychological therapist reacts to the above-mentioned client behaviours in a disapproving and/or morally challenging manner, then this opportunity may be decreased. Therapists need to be able to put their emotional reactions to the side when working with these clients.

Treatment based on formulation

Treatment interventions need to be based on a formulation. This is a 'pocket-size' theory explaining how the client's problems emerged and how they still are maintained.

To understand the emergence and maintenance of problems we like to work with the 'BASIC-ID'-model (Lazarus, 1981) and specifically for a maintenance cycle we like to use a SORCC model (Goldfried, 2003; Nezu and Lombardo, 2004; Eells, 2006; Brown-Chidsey, 2005; Mash and Barkley, 2007; Sturmey, 2007) as discussed in Chapter 3 on assessment and formulation.

Sequence of Interventions

Clients with personality problems take their personality problems into the therapeutic setting. They do not put their personality problems on hold because they are talking to a therapist. A first objective of therapy is to ameliorate the counter-therapeutic behaviours this client engages in. Counter-therapeutic behaviours are those that the client engages in that make doing therapy more difficult. These could be around time-keeping, pro-social behaviour in session (allowing the therapist to finish, absence of abusive language, doing homework tasks, arriving on time for sessions) or behaviours outside the session (self-harm, suicide attempts, other harm and other illegal activities). Doing CBT with a client who constantly talks over the therapist and does not do any of the agreed tasks is impossible. Clients who react to all negative feelings with self-harm and the threat of suicide will make life very difficult for the therapist. It is therefore vital to first of all problematise these behaviours and subsequently provide the client with tools to stop them.

Counter-therapeutic behaviours

Problematising counter-therapeutic behaviours is essential and therapists have to be brave and accept that clients who are not willing to address these issues are not suitable for CBT. This does not mean that the therapist should stop seeing these clients (that depends on the setting you work in) but that it would be wrong to pretend that therapy and change is possible when the client is still engaging in behaviour that makes therapy impossible. The clinician may need to shift from a cure approach to a care approach, and do so openly with the client.

Clients can behave in a counter-therapeutic manner during the sessions. Clients can be so talkative that the therapist can't get a word in edgeways. Clients can also be uncommunicative and answers can be monosyllabic. Another problem can be that the client uses excessive abusive, racist and/or threatening language. We suggest the following strategies for these problems.

Discuss it with the client

When a therapist observes problems with a client's behaviour in the session, it may be a good idea to put this as an issue on the agenda, either in the ongoing session if the issue is an urgent one, or a subsequent session. In such a discussion it is extremely important that the therapist uses optimal communication to get the message across and does not resort to statements such as: 'You always …', 'You deliberately sabotage …', 'You are so rude/racist/ abusive …' It is important to treat this as a moment to give the client some specific feedback, whereby the therapist states exactly what the behaviour is that he/she finds counter-therapeutic ('I have noticed that during sessions you are driven to talk so much that I find it difficult to respond. If I can't respond in a timely manner to what you are saying therapy will become ineffective') and suggests new behaviour for the client ('It would be helpful if you could stop talking when I want to say something. As you seem so driven, I will raise my hand when I need to speak and I would like you to stop talking then. Can we agree on that?').

Using non-verbal signals to help the client focus

Sometimes the clients are so involved in their stories that they find it difficult to stop talking. Agreeing a non-verbal signal might help, but sometimes the therapist needs a more drastic non-verbal gesture. When basic non-verbal gestures don't work, we are inclined to use the strategy of raising our note-pad and blocking eye-contact between client and therapist, while saying in a kind voice: 'If I can just interrupt you there.' Most clients are startled and stop briefly; we then thank them for stopping and continue with what we want to discuss.

Dividing sessions into shorter periods

Whether it is talking too much, talking too little, abusive language; a good strategy is to divide the session as a whole into segments of 15 minutes and use the last five minutes of each period to evaluate how the previous period has gone. Here the therapist has to keep in mind the laws of learning: model desirable behaviour, reward desirable behaviour and perhaps practise desirable behaviour. During the brief evaluation moments the therapist and client would review the previous ten minutes and check how the therapy interfering behaviours have occurred or not.

Lack of collaboration from client

Lack of collaboration will be mainly obvious when a client does not complete the inter-session tasks that the therapist and client have agreed on at the end of each session.

Discussion with the client

The starting point is again to have a discussion with the client about the lack of completed homework tasks. Once again the therapist has to use optimal communication and state the facts, without going into accusing the client. (so don't ask 'Why ...?' but ask 'What were the obstacles for you ...?'). This discussion could lead to a problem-solving session where client and therapist brainstorm about how to overcome the obstacles to completing homework.

The following interaction is an example of such a discussion. The problem is Claire's lack of completing between session tasks.

T:	Our first point on the agenda today is to look at how the therapy is going and whether you are making the progress you want to make.
Claire:	That sounds like a good plan as I am finding that you really are not helping me. I still feel just as miserable now as I felt when I started therapy.
T:	That is a very good point. Therapy is supposed to make you feel better and you are saying that you have not noticed any improvement?
Claire:	That is correct – people treat me just as badly as before and I still feel very depressed and anxious.
T:	I have looked through my notes and seen that over the last six sessions we have discussed mainly your low mood and depression and each session we agreed certain small tasks that you would complete between the sessions.
Claire:	Yes, but they didn't work, not at all ...
T:	Let's see what you make of this. Over the last six weeks, the tasks we agreed would have required you to do a small task each day and six weeks is 42 days, which means 42 tasks. How often do you think you would have needed to do the tasks in order for therapy to work?
Claire:	Well, I think at least half the time ...
Therapist:	Good point – at least half the time. Unfortunately, if we look at the record you kept, your completion of the tasks was only about 15 per cent of the time, so what do you make of that?
Claire:	So now you are saying it is my fault. I just knew it – I can't do anything right, it always goes wrong for me ...
	(Continued)

(Continued)

T:	Remember that I explained to you a while ago the magnetic force of personality problems: we know what is the right thing to do, but we still do the wrong thing. In your situation, you knew the tasks were the right thing to do, but your personality problems pulled you in the other direction. It means we underestimated the strength of the personality problem. And it may mean that our first work may need to be on helping you to become better at completing tasks that are beneficial for you? What do you think?
Claire:	I always have found it very difficult to do things that are good for me, if they cost an effort … I just give up and stop.
T:	That is a really good example of the pulling power of personality problems. How do you react when things start to cost an effort?
Claire:	Well, I just feel it is too hard, that it is unfair that I have to work so hard and that other people have it so easy …
T:	It is too hard, other people have it easy and it is unfair; thinking this seems to lead to giving up or not even trying – do I understand that right?
Claire:	Yes, I give up easily or don't even try.
T:	How do you think this will impact on therapy?
Claire:	Not very well. I know therapy is difficult so I will give up easily. I told you it would be too hard for me!
T:	Any idea what other people do when they are confronted with tasks that they see as too hard and costing too much effort?
Claire:	No, because things seem to be easy for most people.
T:	Let me ask you something. You have gone shopping in the supermarket and have five bags full of groceries. You live in an apartment without a lift and need to take the groceries up five flights of stairs. You can't take five bags all at once, so what would you do?

Asking for smaller acts of collaboration

The therapist can set smaller but still meaningful tasks for the client to complete. Important here is that the therapist has a strategy in place regarding the chronology of homework tasks. Nothing is more discouraging for clients than completing homework that seems to have no connection with what is done in therapy.

More in-session work

When clients do not complete homework tasks, the temptation is to give them more homework tasks in order to maintain pace and momentum in therapy. This will be counterproductive, as the client did not complete the smaller task in the first place. Some clients may find it just impossible for whatever reason to do any between-session tasks. It may be a good idea to do more of the work during sessions instead of between the sessions.

Written agreements

The between-session tasks are here written up as an agreement between client and therapist. Such an agreement would outline exactly *what* the task is and what the *purpose* of the task is, and predict *roadblocks* to completion, *strategies* to resolve the roadblocks and what to do in case of *difficulties*.

Self-destructive behaviours

Self-destructive behaviours by clients are one of the most difficult issues to deal with by therapists. These can be deliberate self-harming, high-risk-taking behaviours and para-suicidal behaviours. Behaviours that leave dramatic signs can be especially disturbing for clinicians (bandages, scars). These obvious signs often have a strong impact on the therapist, ranging from anger towards their client to feelings of despair and clinical incompetence. It is important to continue to see these behaviours, however dramatic and dangerous, as just that: behavioural excesses.

Discussion with the client

It is important to have a discussion with the client about these self-destructive behaviours. It is wise to point out that they need to become a first port of call to change, as it will be very difficult to engage in any meaningful change if these are kept in place. This means that the therapist may need to increase the 'problem validity' of these behaviours as clients often perceive them as 'normal' and not problematic ('just something I do to relieve tension'). Using motivational interviewing strategies and weighing up the pros and cons of the self-destructive behaviours can help to increase the problem validity of self-destructive behaviours. The therapist needs to refrain from strong moral statements such as: 'It is simply wrong what you do to yourself' or demands 'You just have to stop this or else ...' The discussion with the client is intended to 'problematise' the self-destructive behaviour, so it can be put on the problems list and goals can be set regarding this behaviour. In the paragraph on self-management techniques we will review specific strategies to counter these self-destructive behaviours.

Treatment-undermining and/or sabotaging beliefs

'It won't work anyway', 'I have tried everything', 'I have seen so many therapists' and other such statements are indicative of treatment-undermining beliefs. Clients with beliefs like this may be compliant for a short period with the therapy but will be inclined to drop out with the first difficulty or setback. Statements such as the above mentioned are indications that therapy-undermining beliefs are at work. The therapist needs to address these as soon as possible, either immediately or put them on the agenda for a subsequent session.

Discussion leading to giving therapy the 'benefit of the doubt'

Discussing these beliefs does not have the aim of changing the client's mind from 'therapy sucks' to 'therapy is great'. The therapist should have a much more limited goal in mind and that is that attending therapy is not going to make things worse for the client. The client is invited to give CBT the benefit of the doubt.

Using the formulation

In general it is wise to try and avoid having detailed discussions about the benefits of therapy *before* the therapist has completed the assessment and has been able to compose a formulation on the client's problems. Armed with a cognitive behavioural formulation and the relevant maintenance cycles, the first port of call is to help the client understand the mechanisms of his/her problem development and maintenance. Once this is understood, it is easier to explain how specific CBT interventions will break the various maintenance cycles.

This is what we said about Claire:

> Childhood abuse and a harsh upbringing instilled beliefs about mistrust, abuse and abandonment in Claire. In combination with being very unskilled in communication this results in fraught interpersonal relationships. This means that Claire seldom gets what she wants from life and other people. This missing out has now led to an entitlement belief, which means that she perceives all interpersonal relationships as a test for this belief. She dictates interpersonal relationships and interprets others not wanting to go along with that as abuse and abandonment. When she perceives abandonment or abuse, she reacts with strong negative feelings of either anger or anxiety. Engaging in high-risk behaviours is Claire's strategy to reduce the impact of these negative feelings. She has only excessive drinking of alcohol as an alternative to high-risk behaviours in dealing with negative affect.

From this brief summary it is clear that there are several points where interventions could have an impact on the maintenance cycle:

- Learning to express negative feelings, positive feelings and positive requests for change in a pro-social manner.
- Teaching her alternative ways of thinking when she interprets normal interpersonal interactions as abandonment and abuse.
- Teaching her to develop an alternative assertive right perspective as opposed to her entitlement belief.

Explaining this to clients and using diagrams, metaphors and other visual methods to highlight the disruptive impact of new skills on old problem-producing maintenance cycles will have a beneficial impact on the client's belief that therapy will work.

Advantages and disadvantages

Often clients don't want to give therapists the benefit of the doubt and want to be certain from the start that therapy will be successful. If the therapist has nothing to work with (e.g. the assessment and formulation are not complete and therefore any explanation would be a blind one) then a very pragmatic approach may be used: list advantages and disadvantages of attending six sessions with the therapist, just to complete the assessment. For many colleagues, six sessions for an assessment will seem far too many. We would disagree: people with personality problems have complicated and intricate problems. To compose a decent formulation takes time and effort. Therapists who skip this phase will do so to their detriment. We have to learn that doing CBT is like the work of a sharp-shooter: we need to position ourselves carefully, assess which circumstances are relevant and then assess them all, before taking aim carefully … as cognitive behaviour therapists we don't shoot from the hip! In situations where the therapist is 'forced' to deal with the issue that 'therapy will not work for me' before having completed the formulation it may be a good idea to check with the client what he/she perceives the disadvantages are of attending six sessions with this therapist. More often than not the client may come up with disadvantages such as: 'Changing will be hard and difficult', 'I will learn negative things about myself' and 'What if I change but other people don't?' We repeat ourselves: the aim is not to provide a shining example of how fantastic CBT is, but to bring the client to a point where he/she is prepared to give attending a limited number of CBT sessions the benefit of the doubt. During these discussions the therapist adopts the motivational interviewing style as discussed in Chapter 7.

The SORCC as the cornerstone of CBT with personality disorders

We introduced the SORCC model in Chapter 3 as a way of understanding the client's problems. Now we would like to postulate this structure as the basic structure in which to discuss and review all problems the client presents. The advantage of using one structure of analysis is that both client and therapist will – over time – get very good at using it. We like it because it provides us with a structure that enables us to understand 'where the problem lies' in any given situation.

Self-management strategies are required when the client responds with self-defeating or self-destructive behaviour to specific internal or external stimuli. They are also required when the client habitually engages in these behaviours. For instance:

- Being rejected for promotion resulted in getting drunk and driving while intoxicated.
- Being bored resulted in a period of serious self-harm.
- Having an argument with partner results in destroying furniture.
- Daily drinking too much.
- Regular unhelpful substance abuse.

Cognitive interventions are needed when goal attainment is interfered with by strong negative feelings as a result of unhelpful/irrational thinking. For example:

- Believing that people *should* treat the client as special.
- Believing that everyone is always going to reject the client.
- Believing that the worst will happen.

Skills training is needed when the client finds it difficult to engage in certain helpful and pro-social behaviours such as problem solving or communication skills.

Behavioural activation is needed when the lifestyle of the client is counterproductive and unbalanced. For instance:

- Client's life only consists of duties and no leisure.
- Client's life only consists of leisure.
- No satisfying activities in client's life.
- Client's life is too sedentary.

The SORCC model can be used, simply, by inviting the client to review problems in this format. An example of a discussion leading to a SORCC analysis is shown in Table 6.1. Based on this SORCC analysis we concluded that the client (with a diagnosis of borderline personality disorder) needed to learn effective communication skills at work (expressing negative feelings), needed to learn to respond with self-calming strategies when feeling angry and stressed, and needed to learn 'stop-and-think' when feeling very angry.

By using the SORCC model to address all problems the therapist establishes a habit and clients will, after a while, start to bring their own SORCCs to the sessions.

Self-management: alternative behaviours, learning self-soothing, gradual reduction

Once the self-destructive behaviours have been problematised, the best approach is a self-management approach (Watson and Tharp, 2006). This approach can be used for problem excesses such as self-harm, high-risk behaviours, drinking alcohol and substance abuse but also for habitual behavioural deficits (such as self-care and self-soothing).

Table 6.1

Who	Verbatim
T	The next point on the agenda is what happened on Tuesday evening. Would it be ok if we talked about that?
C	It was horrible, I really completely lost it …
T	It was a horrible experience and you felt you completely lost it. What I would suggest is that we discuss what happened following the model that we have used before, the SORCC model, which means that I will have to ask you questions. Would that be ok?
C	As long as it helps me not to do this again.
T	Excellent, so you are already focusing on how to prevent this horrible thing happening in the future. The SORCC will help us to decide what you need to learn and do different to prevent this from happening again. So shall we start?
C	Ok
T	Can you tell me a bit about what happened on Tuesday, just talk me briefly through your day, up until the moment when the horrible thing happened.
C	Well, the horrible thing was that I completely lost it with Bill my fiancé. I screamed and shouted at him and poured wine all over his best suit and then I locked myself in the bathroom with a bottle of gin.
T	So you lost it with Bill and how had your day been before that?
C	I had been at work and worked non-stop from 7.30 in the morning until 7 at night. Running around, organising people, constantly taking care of others, correcting their mistakes, but that all went fine.
T	So during the day everything was perfect and you were very happy? [*using an overshooting to elicit from clients possible problems that occurred during the day and were not dealt with*]
C	No, far from it, because people give me more and more work, I could not stop for lunch and could not do what I planned to do, so I got behind. So by the end of the day I was angry and wound up.
T	Can I conclude from the way you talk about this that this irritation and anger is not expressed in any way when you are at work?
C	No, I can't do that, I am too afraid I might lose it completely like I did with Bill.
T	And then you came home?
C	Yes, I came home exhausted, hungry and there was Bill watching some stupid programme on TV. He said that he had expected me home around 6 (I arrived home around 8) and that he had put a salad for me in the fridge. And …
T	If I can just stop you there. So the Situation, you know the first step in the SORCC, is that you arrive home, tired, angry with the people at work, Bill is watching TV and tells you there is a salad for you in the fridge. How did you react to that?
C	I went to the kitchen, took the salad-bowl out of the fridge and threw it at the TV, then I took the bottle of red wine to his suit and poured it over the suit! And all the while I was screaming at him.
T	So you threw the salad at the TV and poured the wine over his clothes. What was happening inside you when you were doing this?
C	I was so very tense and angry. I thought this bastard is taking advantage of me as well, a salad, does he think I don't deserve a real meal. I am not letting him get away with this.

In this approach the client will go through the following steps:

a   Monitoring of the self-destructive behaviour. Here the client is asked to keep a log of the self-destructive behaviour; depending on frequency and client motivation the client can be asked to keep a log that includes time of day, actual behaviour, behavioural/emotional/

cognitive/environmental antecedents and consequences. If the frequency of the behaviour is very low, the client can be asked to keep a record of the desire to engage in the behaviour and rate this desire on a 0 to 10 point scale.

b Goal setting for self-destructive behaviour. Based on the established frequency of the self-destructive behaviour the client is subsequently asked to start making a reduction plan. The best way to work such a plan is to get the client to set *maximum* behavioural frequency goals for meaningful chunks of time (which depend on the frequency of the self-destructive behaviour), days that are completely free of self-destructive behaviour and identified rewards for complying with the identified goals. In addition the client and therapist identify new rules that will govern the self-destructive behaviour. The self-management plan is very similar to that of a reduction plan used in overcoming addictive behaviours (Feldhege, 1979).

Behaviours that clients do too often are frequently no longer ruled by rules and regulations that govern such behaviours for other people; while behaviours that the client engages in too infrequently are restrained by an excess of very rigid rules. For instance drinking alcohol for a client with borderline personality disorder may be governed by one rule: 'If I want it, I need it and I have to have it'; while doing something nice for herself may be governed by restrictions such as: 'Only really deserving people can do this.' New rules restricting drinking alcohol could be: 'I don't drink alcohol before 10 am; I don't drink after 7 pm.' New rules promoting pro-social behaviours can be: At the end of every part of the day (morning, afternoon, evening) I do something nice for myself: read my book, listen to music, go for a walk or have a relaxing bath.

c Goal setting and reward planning. Many clients with personality disorders have been struggling to change their behaviours for a long time, often with no or limited success. The approach suggested here is to base the goal setting on successive approximation, whereby the client works towards the end goal in small and manageable steps. At the same time, the client needs to design rewards for the effort that he/she puts into the project. Each intermediate goal that is achieved should result in a small reward for the client. These can vary from saying well done to oneself to small gifts.

d Identifying the function of the self-destructive behaviour *and* acquiring alternative behaviour to fulfil this function. Based on the monitoring of the self-destructive behaviour in combination with antecedents and consequences, the therapist and client will be able to identify the use and function of the behaviour. Is it to avoid negative feelings or circumstances or is it to achieve positive consequences or both? Once this is known, client and therapist can brainstorm how the client can achieve the same effect with more adaptive and less self-destructive behaviours. Sometimes the client may not have these behaviours/skills in their repertoire and they may need to be practised in the session (self-calming, self-soothing, compassionate self-talk). It may also be necessary to deviate from the self-management plan and teach the client different skills first before progressing further with the self-management plan.

e Goal setting for alternative behaviour. These alternative behaviours are intended to replace the self-destructive behaviour, but the therapist can give the therapy an extra boost by getting the client to practise the alternative behaviour several times per day, even when there is no need for them. A frequency per day can be agreed as well as rules and regulations governing the new behaviour.

f Evaluation. Client and therapist evaluate the progress in sessions, based on the record keeping of the client.

The self-management approach can also be used for behavioural deficits: self-calming behaviour, self-soothing behaviours or compassionate self-talk. The process is the same. It starts with record keeping of actual doing of the behaviour and record keeping of opportunities to engage in the behaviour as well as situations in which the behaviour needed to be executed. This is followed by goal setting and introducing more permissive rules regarding these positive and pro-social behaviours.

Cognitive Interventions

Many clients with personality problems will put not being able to deal with strong negative feelings high on their list of problems that need resolving. Based on the premise that negative affect is strongly influenced by thinking, an essential intervention is the daily thought record (DTR). With the DTR the client learns to change the unhelpful and irrational thinking into more helpful and rational thinking. The effect of this will be a reduction of the negative affect and an increased ability to engage in pro-social behaviour. The CBT model assumes that irrational thoughts influence negative affect and that this negative affect can be instrumental in promoting maladaptive behaviours or blocking pro-social behaviours.

Working with the DTR assumes three things:

1 The client has been introduced to the CBT model of psychological problems and wants to give working in that model a chance.
2 The therapist has explained the formulation to the client (explaining how the problems got established and how they are maintained).
3 Client and therapist have identified problems and goals to work on and reduction of negative affect was one of the goals.

Intermezzo

What strikes us time and time again is how experienced cognitive behaviour therapists get 'lost' when working with clients who have personality problems. The client's presentation with visible problems (bandages and/or scars) or the client's demanding behaviour and strong expression of negative affect seem to make therapists think that evidence-based strategies no longer apply. In working with personality issues it is very important to 'hold the line': follow evidence-based guidelines and do not let the client's presentation, however sad or distressing, seduce you to do otherwise.

Intermezzo 2

We see the DTR as the second cornerstone of CBT with personality disorder, the first one being the SORCC model. Not because it will resolve all problems, but because it will unearth further problems that stand in the way of change.

Conducting thought records will provide the information regarding roadblocks towards resolving the problems. Clients experiencing high levels of negative affect may lead an unbalanced lifestyle (activity scheduling is needed). The client may not be able to engage in adaptive behaviours because they lack the skills or predict negative consequences (skills training and behavioural experiments are needed). The client may not be able to curb the strong negative automatic thoughts because there are maladaptive beliefs at play (belief change strategies).

DTR

The DTR is introduced to the client as a skill that the client can learn to reduce the impact of negative feelings and enable the client better to engage in desirable behaviours (Davidson, 2007). There are many variations of DTRs available in the literature. We particularly like the one presented here, which we have developed over the years. The good thing about it is that it can be explicitly taught to clients in three steps: in step 1 the client learns to describe the situations as they occur at the moment; in step 2 the client analyses the current situation; and in step 3 the client focuses on change.

Learning to do DTRs is only the start of the process. The more important task is to be able to access the rational thoughts next time when the client is exposed to a similar situation.

Accessing the new rational thoughts

Learning to recognise irrational thinking and replace it with more rational thinking during therapy sessions is only the first step. In the actual situation that triggered the strong negative feelings and/or maladaptive behaviours it will be much more difficult to apply this new skill. This is the moment when the DTR work is tested! We use the following methods to prepare the client for this.

Repetition

When we have identified the new rational thoughts and the client believes them to be true for more then 50 per cent of the time then we can ask the client to put these new rational thoughts on small cue cards and carry these cue cards with them at all times. We then would ask the client to read the new rational thoughts to themselves before any ordinary activity they do with a high frequency: before having a cup of tea/coffee; before getting in the car, before going into a meeting, before answering the next email. This is based on the Premack principle (Premack, 1959). High-frequency behaviours act as reinforcements for-low frequency behaviours – and, as we all know, reinforced behaviours are more likely to occur.

The client can give this repetition a bit more spice and also involve other parts of the brain, not just the rational – frontal cortex – thinking part of the brain by practising saying the rational thoughts out loud with various emotional intonations with accompanying facial expressions. This ensures that the new rational thoughts also create links with emotional parts of the brain and emotional states. It will be helpful to practise this in the sessions and it may be needed that the therapist models the various expressions.

Externalising of dialogue

The internal debate between 'irrational' and 'rational' thinking is here externalised. The best way to start this process is again to get the rational thoughts on a cue card and then client and therapist conduct a role-play. The therapist plays the role of the client's irrational thinking while the client holds the fort for the rational perspective. The therapist needs to keep a careful eye on client's reactions and stop the role-play if the client starts to waver, e.g. the rational thoughts crumble. When this happens, stop the role-play and go back to the drawing board: find more, better rational alternatives. A good starting point for these exercises is for the client to describe what factually happened. Here is the 'externalising of dialogue' Claire did with her therapist:

Claire:	I arrived at work, as per usual, around 8.30 am and walked into the open plan office and said 'Good morning'. Sally and Peter were standing at the coffee machine and said 'Good morning, Claire!' The others (Jack, Allan, Moira and Gavin) did not respond to my good morning.
T:	But that is just horrible, they deliberately ignored you, the bastards!
Claire:	Well, you could be over-generalising there. It is true they did not greet me, but they were all on the phone and Gavin was also being talked to by his PA.
T:	But still when someone says good morning and colleagues and the boss don't respond, that must be a sign that they are planning something behind your back. You are probably going to get fired. How can you accept being treated so unjustly!
Claire:	Mindreading and fortune-telling, that is what you are doing. I don't have any evidence to support the idea that I will get fired or that people are planning something behind my back. Everyone has been friendly and my performance reviews with Gavin have been ok to very good.
T:	But people stab you in the back when you least expect it.

The therapist really tries all the 'dirty' debating tricks to unsettle the client's rational resolve (because that is what client's own mind will do).

'Yesterday-ing'

The song 'Yesterday' made famous by The Beatles is well suited for this process. Here therapist and client, or the clients by themselves, change the text of the song. The original text is replaced by a text describing how to go from the irrational thoughts to the rational thoughts. If the song is chosen wisely, e.g. a song that the client really likes and can remember easily, then doing this will be of invaluable assistance in helping the client recall the rational thoughts at crucial emotional moments.

The client can actually sing the song, in private, in public or record it and bring it to the session. The aim is to anchor the new rational thoughts in the client's brain so they can be reproduced when needed.

DTRs Instructions

Table 6.2

Step 1: That is how things are NOW!

1. What is the situation?

Here the client is invited to record the situation he/she was in when the negative feelings were very strong. Client describes, when, where, with whom, what they were doing and any other relevant circumstances.

2. How did you feel in that situation and how strong were the feelings on a scale of 0–100?

The client writes down the negative feelings experienced. It is very important to teach the client here to write down feelings and not sensation or words describing heightened arousal. Clients are also invited to record the strength of their feelings. So NOT: upset, uptight, stressed, BUT: anxious, depressed, guilty.

3. What do you do that really does not work to get over the problem?

Here the client writes down the behaviour they engage in as a result of the negative feelings. This is sometimes difficult, especially when the client does not seem to engage in any behaviour (see examples) and abstains from pro-social behaviour.

4. What are your thoughts in that situation, especially thoughts that promote the feelings under 2 (please number these thoughts)?

This is the real one! This is what it is all about. Here the therapist needs to get the client to disclose their thinking. Often crafty Socratic dialogue is necessary and continually checking whether the thoughts match the emotions.

5. How much do you believe these thoughts to be true? (Give each of the thoughts a rating from 0 (= not true at all) to 100 (= completely true).)

Each of the thoughts needs to be checked out with respect to how much the client believes the thought to be true in the specific situation (as a flexibility of mind check). The therapist could ask the client how much they believe the thought while sitting in the consulting room of the therapist; if there is a discrepancy this can be worked with.

Table 6.3

Step 2: Your self-analysis of how things are

The description of situation will be the same.

1. Do you want to feel like this?

This question is a motivation check. Sometimes clients are 'attached' to their negative feelings and don't really feel motivated to give them up.

2. How helpful is it to behave like this?

Here the therapist checks with the client what the pragmatic value is of the behaviour triggered by the emotions and thoughts.

(Continued)

Table 6.3 *(Continued)*

3. Now analyse your thoughts:

a. Is this thought a fact or is it your opinion?
b. Does this thought help you feel the way you want to feel and behave the way you want to behave?
c. Is this thought an example of (1) Demanding, (2) Catastrophising, (3) Low-frustration tolerance, (3) 'Self/other downing' or any of the other thinking errors?

See separate page.

Table 6.4

Step 3: This is how I WANT things to be.

The situation is the same. Beware that the client does not puts changes in the situation so that it becomes easier for her/him to deal with the situation.

1. How would you like to feel in these situations?

This is a very important question. Most clients want to go from a strong negative feeling (very depressed) to a strong positive feeling (very happy). The therapist needs to introduce a reality check here and explain that CBT is not a positive thinking movement. When you feel depressed and you have been feeling like this for many years, to expect that you will feel very happy in similar circumstances is several bridges too far. Here we teach clients that to say that it smells like roses, when 'the shit hits the fan' is highly irrational. When the 'shit hits the fan' it stinks and that is unpleasant, but it is not terrible, it is not a catastrophe.

2. How would you like to behave in these situations?

Here we ask the client how they would like to behave in the given situation. This may often be a bit of a challenge as the client may have reacted to these situations in this style for a very long time. As result of that they may not be able to imagine that they could react differently. The therapist needs to be guided by the formulation, but also common sense plays an important role.

3. What are alternative factual and helpful thoughts that 'promote' how you would like to behave and would like to feel?

For each of the unhelpful thoughts the client and therapist need to compose a rational alternative. These rational alternatives need to:

- *Evaluate how bad the actual situation is.*
- *Be based on preferences.*
- *Focus on high frustration tolerance.*
- *Focus on self/other acceptance as fallible human beings.*
- *Be believable by the client.*

4. How much do you believe these new thoughts on a scale of 0–100?

The client rates each of the new thoughts on the 0–100 scale.

5. Go back to box 4 – how much do you believe these thoughts now (rate one a scale from 0–100)?

And again with the original thoughts.

Thinking about your thinking

Table 6.5

Thoughts from box 4	Is this thought a fact or is it your opinion?	Does this thought help you feel the way you want to feel and behave the way you want to behave?	Which Thinking Errors do you recognise in this thought?

(Continued)

Table 6.5 (Continued)

Here the thought is written down. A word of warning about thoughts. Often clients disclose their thoughts to therapists in a sanitised way. The thought might have been: 'Those bastards can drop dead, I hate them and will f*****g destroy them', but the client might say to the therapist: 'It is not very nice that they did that.' It is very important to get clients' real thoughts included in the thought record. Another thought pitfall is when clients write down very moderate thoughts but given their feelings they should have had much stronger thoughts. Socratic dialogue to get the real thoughts is the name of the game.	Here client and therapist check whether the thought was based on facts, i.e. is it a factually true statement?	This focuses on the pragmatic value of the thought. Is the thought helpful in achieving our personal goals, in feeling better or getting along better with people?	Here client and therapist try to 'label' the thought with a thinking error.

An example of a DTR

Table 6.6

Step 1: That is how things are NOW!

What is the situation?

I (Claire) arrive at work in the morning and say 'Good morning everybody' and Gavin, my boss, does not respond. He was in the office with four other people and they all responded.

How did you feel in that situation and how strong were the feelings on a scale of 0–100?

Extremely angry.

What do you do that really does not work to get over the problem?

I went to my office, slammed the door shut and, when no one came to check on me, left work again after 15 minutes. I shouted at my boss: 'If this is how you want to play it so be it. I am going home.' On my way home I bought a couple of bottles of Jack and drank myself silly. Was off work for a week after this binge.

What are your thoughts in that situation, especially thoughts that promote the feelings under 2 (please number these thoughts)?

- The bastard he is ignoring me again.
- He is planning to get me fired, he is so unfair.
- No one can be trusted, he is going to stab me in the back.
- I have to pay him back.
- They should not treat me so badly.

(Continued)

Table 6.6 (Continued)

How much do you believe these thoughts to be true? (Give each of the thoughts a rating from 0 (= not true at all) to 100 (= completely true).)	
The bastard he is ignoring me again.	100
He is planning to get me fired, he is so unfair.	90
No one can be trusted; he is going to stab me in the back.	90
I have to pay him back.	90
They should not treat me so badly.	90

Table 6.7

Step 2: Your self-analysis of how things are

I (Claire) arrive at work in the morning and say 'Good morning everybody' and Gavin, my boss, does not respond. He was in the office with four other people and they all responded.

1. Do you want to feel like this?

No, I don't want to feel like this!

2. How helpful is it to behave like this?

Not really helpful, walking away from the job and calling in sick for a week is not going to do my career prospects any good!

3. Now analyse your thoughts:

   i. Is this thought a fact or is it your opinion?
   ii. Does this thought help you feel the way you want to feel and behave the way you want to behave?
   iii. Is this thought an example of:

      a. Demanding
      b. Catastrophising
      c. Low frustration tolerance
      d. Self/other downing
      e. Any of the other thinking errors

See separate sheet.

Table 6.8

Step 3: This is how I WANT things to be

I (Claire) arrive at work in the morning and say 'Good morning everybody' and Gavin, my boss, does not respond. He was in the office with four other people and they all responded.

1 How would you like to feel in these situations?

Well, fact is I said 'Good morning' and Gavin did not respond (because of my immediate anger I did not notice the circumstances – he was on the phone) So I would like to feel disappointed.

2 How would you like to behave in these situations?

I would want to stay at work and look closer at the situation. If I had done this in the situation we discussed I would have seen that Gavin was rather busy and simply did not notice me coming in and saying 'Good morning'.

(Continued)

Table 6.8 *(Continued)*

3   What are alternative factual and helpful thoughts that 'promote' how you would like to behave and would like to feel?

- ○ *The bastard he is ignoring me again* → <u>He is not greeting me, that is different from ignoring. The man is busy, get real!</u>
- ○ *He is planning to get me fired, he is so unfair.* → <u>I am just making this up, he has never fired me before, so there is no AGAIN. Gavin is in general a firm and fair boss. No indication he is going to fire me.</u>
- ○ *No one can be trusted, he is going to stab me in the back.* → <u>Some people are not trustworthy. So far Gavin has been a fair boss and I have no evidence to support the idea he is not trustworthy!</u>
- ○ *I have to pay him back.* → <u>I can hear the battle drums! There is nothing to pay him back for. These revenge thoughts just make me do stupid things that WILL get me fired!</u>
- ○ *They should not treat me so badly.* → <u>If they would be treating me badly, and they are not, that would be their 'right' and it would be my right to take appropriate legal action!</u>

4   How much do you believe these new thoughts 0–100?
- ○ <u>He is not greeting me, that is different from ignoring. The man is busy, get real! = 75</u>
- ○ <u>I am just making this up, he has never fired me before, so there is no AGAIN. Gavin is in general a firm and fair boss. No indication he is going to fire me. = 80</u>
- ○ <u>Some people are not trustworthy. So far Gavin has been a fair boss and I have no evidence to support the idea he is not trustworthy! = 70</u>
- ○ <u>I can hear the battle drums! There is nothing to pay him back for. These revenge thoughts just make me do stupid thing that WILL get me fired! = 100</u>
- ○ <u>If they would be treating me badly, and they are not, that would be their 'right' and it would be my right to take appropriate legal action! = 90</u>

5   Go back to box 4 – how much do you believe these thoughts now (rate one a scale from 0–100)?

- ○ *The bastard he is ignoring me again.* = 25
- ○ *He is planning to get me fired, he is so unfair.* = 25
- ○ *No one can be trusted, he is going to stab me in the back.* = 20
- ○ *I have to pay him back.* = 0
- ○ *They should not treat me so badly.* = 20

Thinking about your thinking

Table 6.9

Thoughts from box 4.	Is this thought a fact or is it your opinion?	Does this thought help you feel the way you want to feel and behave the way you want to behave?	Which Thinking Errors do you recognise in this thought?
The bastard he is ignoring me again.	Well, he was on the phone and Sally (his PA was talking to him). He	Not helpful, it made me very angry.	Over-generalising.

(Continued)

Table 6.9 *(Continued)*

	probably did not notice me. This is a belief, not a fact.		
He is planning to get me fired, he is so unfair.	I have no evidence that Gavin is planning to fire me. My last performance review was ok. This is an opinion.	Not helpful, makes me feel afraid and when I get afraid I get angry at the people who I think make me afraid!	Mind reading.
No one can be trusted; he is going to stab me in the back.	Many people at work have been rather reliable and helpful. There have been people in the past who treated me badly, but I have no real evidence that any of my colleagues or Gavin is planning to do so. Opinion.	No, makes me angry and filled with self-pity	Over-generalising, fortune telling.
I have to pay him back.	This is a revenge thought – even if Gavin was planning to fire me, it is not the law of the universe that I would HAVE to pay him back. Opinion.	This really fuels my revenge fantasies. Not helpful at all.	Demanding thinking.
They should not treat me so badly.	There is no law in the universe that dictates how people should or should not treat me. Opinion.	Anger- and revenge-provoking thought.	Demanding thinking.

The Behaviour in DTRs

The question 'How would you like to behave if the situation arose again?' can be met by clients with disbelief. They might say things like 'Of course I could ask for a day off, but the reaction of my boss would be terrible'; or 'I would like to speak up for myself and disagree with them, but I would not know how to!' The therapist has uncovered a new roadblock to change in the client. Informed by the client's reaction to the idea of 'new' behaviour, the therapist can suggest interventions to overcome this roadblock.

If the client's reaction is one of fear for predicted negative consequences then a behavioural experiment is an option, while if the objections are based on not knowing how, then skills training is indicated. Sometimes the predicted consequences are mildly negative, but as a result of client's lack of problem-solving skills they become very negative. For instance, for Joanne, asking for a day off work so she could prepare her house move became a big problem. She planned to move house in the busiest period of the accountancy firm's she worked for and her boss had said no to a previous request. Joanne interpreted this as a complete definitive veto on having time off to prepare her house move. She could not resolve this problem, so we taught her the problem solving process. This resulted in her wanting to ask the help of an older colleague (how to do this required some skills training) and accompanied by this colleague she approached the boss again and explained her predicament (how to do this needed some skills training). This resulted in the employer suggesting a specific day on which she could take the day off and suggested that if colleagues wanted to help her they could leave work early on that day.

The DTR is really the centrepiece of working with clients with personality problems as all cognitive, emotional and behavioural problems will come to the foreground in carefully done DTRs.

It is not straightforward!

Don't expect this process of cognitive restructuring to be smooth sailing. Many thought records and many repetitions of challenging and disputing the same thoughts and beliefs may be necessary – but sometimes disputing seems not to work.

The therapist and client review the client's negative automatic thoughts and both agree that they are not helpful and not based on facts and subsequently the client surprises the therapist by stating that they still believe it is true! We were working with a client with a diagnosis of narcissistic personality disorder on the negative automatic thought: 'Other people have to treat me with special respect.' The client agreed with the therapist that this was not supported by facts, nor was it helpful, but stated that they still believed it to be true. It is very important that the therapist maintains a neutral and Socratic inquisitive style and demonstrates that she/he really is interested in knowing why a client thinks this thought is true. Table 6.1 shows the discussion that we had with the client. Discussion like this needs to be repeated several times, until the client has built up some experiential learning that demonstrates that the new belief is really ok.

Table 6.10

Who	Verbatim
T	Other people have to treat me with special respect – this thought still rings very true for you. Can you tell me a bit more about that?
C	It just feels right. If people don't give me the respect I deserve, I feel lost, lonely …
T	So your emotional reaction is some kind of evidence for you that this thought has a strong reality value?
C	That is exactly right – if it was not true, I wouldn't react as strongly as this. The thought of being treated like some ordinary hick fills me with horror. To be ordinary is to be nothing and I don't want to be nothing.
T	The picture I am getting is that you seem to equal being treated like everyone else as really terrible because it makes you think you are nothing. Can you tell me a bit more about that?

(Continued)

Table 6.10 *(Continued)*

C	Well if people don't treat me special, with special respect then they see me as one of the crowd, a tree in a wood, something that can be overlooked, ignored, trampled on and destroyed. I have to be special to exist.
T	So the chain starts with people not giving you the special treatment, this makes you think that you are nothing and that as one of the crowd you can be treated badly and that leads to you thinking that you only exist when you are treated special?
C	Yes, I feel numb inside when people treat me ordinarily and I feel I come alive when I am treated as special.
T	There is an interesting discrepancy between what your feelings tell you (I need to be treated special) and the result of our previous discussion (all humans are equal and no one deserves special treatment). Holding on to the demand for special treatment seems to have got you into trouble with other people and with the law a couple of times. Accepting equal treatment from other makes you feel bad. Any idea how we can resolve this discrepancy?
C	Perhaps I could learn to react differently when people treat me just like other people, but I don't want to stop believing I am special!

Negative automatic thoughts and beliefs

In the literature about the treatment for personality disorders we often find that it is necessary to aim for schema change or core belief change in order for CBT with personality disordered clients to be effective. We have, however, found no clinical trials supporting this statement. Maladaptive schemas or core beliefs may be influential in causing and maintaining problems of people with personality problems, but this should be 'demonstrated' through therapeutic work. In other words, when we work with thought records to help the clients bring about change in their lives and we notice that certain negative automatic thoughts are frequently returning or we find that there is a commonality in all the cognitions we elicit in the situations we review, then we can hypothesise that there is an underlying belief or core belief at work. This belief may need to be addressed directly when working with thought records produces insufficient change, despite covering the skills deficit issue.

First, the underlying belief needs to be identified. This can be done by using the thought record and adopting the 'downward arrow technique'. When using this technique the therapist acts like a very curious bystander who really wants to know how the client's brain operates, by constantly asking for the meaning if a certain event were to happen:

* If they were to reject you what would that mean for you?
* If she said no, what would that mean to you?
* Why is making a mistake so bad?
* What is so bad about being disapproved of?

Doing this persistently will lead to the client's beliefs, core beliefs and/or rules for living. Once these have been 'found' or established as being instrumental in the client's problems the following steps need to be taken to help the client work towards different, more adaptive beliefs, core beliefs or rules for living:

- Historical perspective.
- Pragmatic perspective.
- Rational perspective.
- Behaviour supporting the rational perspective.

Belief change and a historical perspective

The aim of this step is to assist the client in understanding how he/she learned these beliefs or rules for living. Questions to ask are: 'How did you learn ...?'; 'How did you come to believe ...?'; 'Who taught you ...?' As homework the client can be asked to put in a timeline how this belief has influenced their life. Get the client to answer questions such as: 'Which good and which less good things have happened to you as a result of adopting this belief/rule for living?'

The aim is for client and therapist to understand that these beliefs do not drop out of the sky, but that there is a reason for developing these beliefs – either life's experiences or modelling from parents.

This step is complete when the client can complete the following sentence (or one similar): 'No wonder I developed the belief that XXX, because YYY happened to me and believing XXX seemed to be a logical option, given my life's experiences after that and my current circumstances ZZZ seems to be a more realistic belief.'

Pragmatic perspective

Here client and therapist check out how useful adhering to the belief/rule is *now*. This can be done in the session by checking the advantages and disadvantages of the current belief/rule for living. The aim here is to help the client to come to the conclusion that although this belief may feel familiar, it is not a belief that is advantageous to keep adhering to. The end-point is when the client sees more disadvantages in adhering to the belief then advantages.

Rational perspective

Here client and therapist try to formulate an alternative to the original maladaptive belief or rule for living. Adaptive beliefs need to be based on reality, helpful for goal achievement to the client and believable to the client, just like alternative thoughts in the DTR. Similar strategies to those we discussed for confirming rational thoughts in the client's mind can be used for beliefs: repetition, externalising of dialogues and 'Yesterday-ing'.

Behavioural perspective

Here client and therapist identify specific behaviours that the client can engage in to support the new adopted belief or rule for living. The behaviours will act

INTERVENTIONS FOR (LASTING) CHANGE

as the best confirmations that the new belief is a better bet than the old one. Often this needs to be done in the format of behavioural experiments.

Behavioural Experiments

How to conduct behavioural experiments has been very well described. Behavioural experiments are aimed at testing the client's hypothesised outcome of engaging in certain behaviours:

> 'If I speak up for myself I will be mercilessly criticised.'
> 'If I say no, they will all reject me.'
> 'If I apologise, they will humiliate me.'

The client and therapist prepare carefully what the behaviour is that the client will engage in and work at making the client's prediction as specific as possible (e.g. what will people exactly do to humiliate you?). The client then executes the experiment and the results are followed by an evaluation between client and therapist. The focus in this evaluation is whether the hypothesised outcome happened. For clients with personality problems there are a few 'specials' that the therapist may need to pay attention to:

- Beware of skills deficits in executing the behaviours. It may be prudent to role-play situations before asking the client to test things out outside the therapy session. It would not be the first time that what a client considers to be a polite request is in fact a rude demand.
- Beware of catastrophic misinterpretations by the client. Client may interpret a polite refusal as a massive rejection. Therapist can prevent this from happening by investigating in detail the predictions of the client.
- Beware of 'yes, but ...' from the client. Here the client does not really go along with your reasoning and you may need to review his/her 'but' with a DTR.

Skills training

We consider the following five skills to be very important and frequent deficits in people with personality problems:

- Active listening
- Expressing positive feelings
- Expressing negative feelings
- Making positive requests
- Problem-solving skills

In dialectical behaviour therapy (Linehan et al., 1999) skills training is one of the pillars of the treatment programme. We cannot stress enough the importance of this as part of a treatment for personality disorders. We mean *real* training, whereby client and therapist practise the skills in various role-played situations. It is extremely important to include actual practice in the treatment especially for clients with personality disorders whose ways of doing life are so entrenched and rigid.

Lacking communication

Our communication is our tool to interact with the world and the other people in it. Communication is what we use when we want other people to know that they have done something that we really liked or when they are doing something we don't like. We also use communication to 'understand' other people. People with personality problems often lack these skills or under-use them.

We suggest a uniform strategy of teaching these skills. In step 1 the client and therapist discuss the skill and design a checklist for this skill (the checklists are based on the elements listed in the remainder of this chapter). The next step is that the therapist demonstrates the skill to the client in the form of a carefully scripted role-play. It is important for the client to recognise the various elements of the skill. In step 3 the client is invited to practise the skill in the session in a role-play. Step 4 is to practise the skill in real life with other people that the client feels he/she can practise with easily. Step 5 is in-session practice of the skill in difficult situations and step 6 is to practise in real life in difficult situations.

Active listening

Listening is an important skill: it allows us to understand what other people are really saying to us. It prevents us from jumping to conclusions without having checked out whether we heard things correctly. For many clients with personality disorders this is an essential skill to learn: hearing what really is being said instead of jumping to conclusions.

These are the elements of this communication skill.

Non-verbal

- Make eye contact.
- An attentive facial expression.
- A kind tone of voice.
- Use plenty of 'ah ha's.

Verbal

- Repeating certain key words.
- Paraphrasing what the other person has told you (content) and how they told you (emotion).
- Using plenty of summaries: simply summarising what the other person has told you.
- Asking questions, so you can understand better.

Too often when we are pretending to listen to another person, we are just preparing our own counter-argument. Listening is really trying to understand where the other person is coming from.

Expressing positive feelings

Expressing positive feelings is the tool we have to let other people know when they have done something to please us. It is *the* tool to reward other people for behaving in a way we want them to behave. By being appreciative and nice about it, they will be inclined to do it more often. The expression of positive feelings also creates a nice atmosphere in the moment.

When we introduce this skill many clients try to convince us it is not necessary. People know that we appreciate them, they tell us, and there is no need to say it. Many clients expect other people to mind read!

These are the elements of this communication skill:

- Look at person, and speak in a friendly way.
- You may smile, shake hands, or make some other warm gesture if that seems right for the situation.
- Tell the person exactly what things they did that pleased you.
- Tell the person exactly how it made us feel when they did that.
- 'I was pleased … I was happy … I enjoyed …'
- 'I was delighted … I was excited … I liked …'

Expressing negative feelings

Many people think that the only way to express negative feelings is to start screaming and shouting, but that is not the case. Expressing negative feelings is extremely important because we let other people know what they have done that caused us to be irritated, hurt, angry, sad or disappointed. This skill can be very well combined with making positive requests.

These are the elements of this communication skill:

- Look at the person and speak in a firm manner.
- Tell them exactly what has triggered your unpleasant feelings.
- Tell them exactly what they did that triggered you to feel what you feel.
- Tell them exactly what you are feeling.
- Use the tone of voice, facial expressions and gestures that convey these feelings.
- Suggest ways that they might help you get rid of these feelings.
- For example, make a positive request or arrange a problem-solving discussion.

Making positive requests

Making a positive request is basically asking another person to change their behaviour:

- Look at the person and speak in a warm tone.
- Tell them exactly what you would like them to do.

- Tell them how you expect to feel when they have done that.
- Use phrases such as:

  - 'I would like you to ...'
  - 'I would be pleased if you would ...'
  - 'I would be grateful if you ...'

No problem solving

Many people lead unhappy and unfulfilled lives because they allow problems to fester and ruin their lives. Most problems can be resolved and will not simply go away through the passage of time.

Problems need to be confronted and resolved. We suggest a four-step approach to problem solving (D'Zurilla and Nezu, 2007):

1 Define the problem and the goal. Here is where you think about what the problem is really and what would be a reasonable solution to the problem. For example: my problem is that I stepped into a big pile of dog-poop and I don't want to smell of poop and make the whole floor in the office dirty. A solution would be if I could clean my shoe.
2 Brainstorm solutions. Brainstorming means just listing all possible solutions, without disregarding any of them. Sometimes they just flow and at other times you will have to think hard. When you have at least four, you make a selection of the best. In the dog-poop example, we could come up with: (1) go back home and change shoes; (2) throw shoes away and buy a new pair; (3) go to the nearest supermarket and get a plastic bag and put it over the poop foot, go to work and wash off in the toilet; (4) clean the shoe as best you can on the street (find some grass, some water, some paper) and go to work as normal. Selecting the best solution is always based on the solution that best reflects your goals. In the dog-poop situation your goals may be not to miss work and not to spend money on new shoes unnecessarily.
3 Selection: in the dog-poop situation, immediate cleaning of my shoes as best as I can clearly has most advantages as, compared to the other solutions, it saves time and money.
4 Implementation: in order to implement the solution, I need to find a way to clean my shoes, perhaps on the curb of the pavement or finding some grass to wipe my shoes clean.

Clients are often surprised at the fact that they can follow a step-by-step process in resolving problems. Their previous strategies had been based on avoidance and/or impulsive action.

Life style imbalance

Many clients with personality problems have developed unhealthy and unbalanced lifestyles. This may lead to depression, chronic boredom and burn-out. Helping clients to adapt a more balanced lifestyle that as a result will reduce certain negative feelings is often a first port of call for therapists. For clients to profit from a psychological therapy such as CBT it will be necessary to develop a balanced lifestyle.

We teach clients activity scheduling in several steps.

Step I: self-monitoring

This is what we tell the client about this:

Self-monitoring simply means observing your pattern of activities. It involves keeping a detailed record of what you do, hour by hour. You can do this in a notebook or diary, or your therapist will give you a special record sheet. Rate your pleasure and satisfaction for each activity on a scale of 0 to 10.

Your record will show you in black and white how you are spending your time, and will make you aware of how much satisfaction and pleasure you get from what you do. You will have a factual record to help you find out more about what is getting in your way, and to form a basis for changing how you spend your time.

We ask clients to keep a record of at least a week of their activities, using the Activity Schedule.

Step 2: planning ahead

This is what we say to the client about this step: 'Now that you can see how you are spending your time, the next step is to plan each day in advance, making sure that you include activities, which will give you a sense of pleasure and satisfaction.'

Intermezzo: what does the client want from life?

This is not an easy question to answer but to make it easier we have designed the following exercise that will help your client to make a start with finding out about this.

Ask the client to imagine they have lived to the ripe old age of 85 and it is their birthday. Today family and friends will be visiting. They will congratulate the client and there will be speeches. You have one question for the client: 'What would you want other people to say about you in these speeches? When they talk about you in these speeches what would you like them to say about you?'

Ask your client to write one such speech. Other people have included things such as hard working, loyal, kind, generous, funny, serious, a good friend and very giving.

In the subsequent session you then list the character traits the client has listed as desirable and make an inventory of which behaviours would demonstrate that someone possesses this trait. These behaviours can then become a guideline for planning activities.

The following is an example of how to guide the client:

Planning ahead means that you are taking control of your life. The plan will prevent you from sinking into a swamp of minor decisions ('What shall I do next?'), and will help you to keep going even when you feel bad. Once the day's activities are laid out in writing, they will seem less overwhelming. You will have broken the day down into a series of manageable chunks, rather than a long shapeless string of time, which you must somehow fill.

Every evening, or first thing in the morning, set aside time to plan the day ahead. Find out which time suits you best to do this, remembering that you are likely to be able to plan most realistically and constructively when you are feeling relatively well and clear-headed. If you find it difficult to remember to make time to plan ahead, give yourself reminder cues. Put up signs around the house, for example, or ask someone to remind you that 7.30 is your time for planning tomorrow. As far as possible, try to ensure that your planning time is not interrupted, and that there are no other pressing demands to distract you. Turn off the television, and take the phone off the hook.

Aim for a balance between pleasure and mastery in your day and remember to include activities based on the person you want to be. If you fill your time with duties and chores, and allow no time for enjoyment or relaxation, you may find yourself feeling tired, resentful and depressed at the end of the day. On the other hand, if you completely ignore things you have to do, you may find your pleasure soured by a sense that nothing has been achieved, and your list of necessary tasks will mount up. You may find it helpful to aim for the pattern of activities you found most rewarding in the past. There is a fair chance that, once you get going, you will find this pattern works for you again.

Encourage yourself by starting the day with an activity that will give you a sense of mastery or pleasure, and that you have a good chance of completing successfully. This is particularly important if you have trouble getting going in the morning. And plan to reward yourself with a pleasurable or relaxing activity when you tackle something difficult. You might, for example, set aside time to have a cup of coffee and listen to your favourite radio programme when you have spent an hour doing housework. Avoid bed. Beds are for sleeping in, not for retreating to during the day. If you need rest or relaxation, plan to achieve it in some other way.

At the end of each day, review what you have done. Take the time to sit down and examine how you spent your day, how much pleasure and mastery you got from what you did and how far you managed to carry out the activities you had planned. This will help you to see clearly how you are spending your time, what room there is for improvement and what changes you might like to make in the pattern of your day.

If you have managed overall to stick to your plan, and have found what you did reasonably satisfying, this gives you something positive to build on. If on the other hand you did not stick to your plan, or you got little satisfaction from what you did, this will give you valuable information about the kind of things that are preventing you from making the most of your time.

Table 6.11

Hour	Monday	Tuesday	Wednesday	Thursday	Friday	Saturday	Sunday
1.							
2.							
3.							
4.							
5.							
6.							
7.							
8.							
9.							
10.							
11.							
12.							
13.							
14.							
15.							
16.							
17.							
18.							
19.							
20.							
21.							
22.							
23.							
24.							

We also instruct the client to go back to the 85th birthday speech and the behaviours we identified from there. We would ask clients to include at least one new activity in their repertoire each week that is evidence of one of the traits they value.

Activity Schedule

The client should write down for each hour their main activity and rate their mood for each hour: −10 = extremely depressed; +10 = extremely elated (see Table 6.11).

Reflection on interventions for lasting change

Helping clients with personality disorders make meaningful and lasting change is not easy. A formulation about the client's problems provides us with a basic map of tasks that need to be achieved. The challenge in working with personality disorder is to establish a therapeutic collaboration with the client that enables the client–therapist team to apply therapeutic interventions effectively and in a meaningful sequence. Applying the SORCC model as a structure with which to 'understand' problems is our way of ensuring that the client truly can become their own best therapist and that interventions are applied comprehensively and correctly:

- Is sufficient attention given to clients' impulsive reaction to certain stimuli?
- Is sufficient attention given to clients' lack of satisfaction and pleasure in life?
- Is sufficient attention given to clients' overwhelming negative feelings and the irrational thinking underpinning these feelings?

The SORCC is helpful in identifying which elements of the problem presentation need to be worked on therapeutically. We reviewed and presented a range of cognitive interventions with the DTR as a core technique. We also reviewed a number of more behavioural interventions such as skills training and activity scheduling.

Understanding Check

Things you should be able to do after reading this chapter:

1 Explain how the SORCC is used as a foundation of CBT with personality disorder, giving one example.
2 Outline the relationship between formulation and treatment plan.
3 Explain what the core intervention in CBT is for personality problems.
4 List examples of counter-therapeutic behaviours.
5 Describe when the therapist needs to address counter-therapeutic behaviours.

7

ENGAGEMENT STRATEGIES

In this chapter you will learn about:

- The stages of change.
- Fundamental motivational interviewing strategies.
- Advanced motivational interviewing strategies.

Motivation for Change

People with personality problems are often not very motivated to change. This could be because their problem behaviours result in too many rewards or because the familiarity of the current situation or it may be connected with being afraid of the unknown that change will bring. These clients are a challenge for psychological therapists.

In this chapter we will describe a strategy that will enable psychological therapists to understand the mechanisms underpinning lacking motivation (the stages of change model). The building blocks of motivation for change are discussed and methods on how to engage with clients so that these building blocks for motivation are strengthened and not dismantled.

Stages of Change

Prochaska et al. (1992) describe a stages of change model. The model describes the journey of a person from being unmotivated to a stage where changes have been made and are now maintained. They postulate that different stages of change demand different engagement strategies (see Figure 7.1).

Precontemplation
During this stage people are not aware they have problems and therefore don't think of change; there is a lack of integrated and accepted personal knowledge of the problems. They might have some form of abstract knowledge that the behaviours they engage in are not ok for people, but for some reason this does not apply to them. Realising that one engages in problematic behaviour does

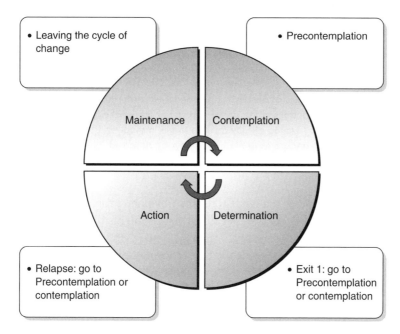

Figure 7.1 Stages of change

not feel good. It is often accompanied by a temporary loss of self-esteem and self-efficacy. This implies that people are likely to defend themselves against the idea of having problems. People tend to have a certain built-in defence mechanism against a decrease in self-esteem and self-efficacy. This defence is stating that nothing is wrong or if there is something that is wrong it doesn't matter.

If a person in pre-contemplation wanted to change anything, this would not be their own behaviour but the behaviour of others.

Obstacles in progressing from pre-contemplation to contemplation are:

- No integrated and personally accepted *knowledge* about the problems; for knowledge to become relevant in influencing attitudes and behaviour it has to be personalised. There is a difference between academic knowledge, e.g. drinking too much is bad for people, and the way I drink is bad for *me*. This knowledge goes beyond abstract knowledge ('People who are angry all the time will have no friends') and needs to be personalised ('I don't have any friends because I am angry and critical with everyone around me').
- A too low level of self-efficacy and *self-esteem* (accepting the knowledge that something is wrong brings the self-esteem and self-efficacy to a critical low threshold.) If you are in a problematic situation (e.g. feeling lonely and being all alone with no friends) that may be a problem to you if you see yourself as deserving better (e.g. being worthwhile enough to have friends). If on the other hand you see yourself as undeserving and worthless (in other words you do not appreciate the value of your good self) then having no friends is just what you deserve. Knowledge about the problems is only effective in stimulating motivation for change if it is combined with a sense that one is worthwhile enough to not have these problems.

- John with a diagnosis of anti-social personality disorder has been arrested (again) for driving under the influence: 'It is not my fault the police are out to get me, they were just waiting for me. This is persecution you know.'
- Belinda with a diagnosis of narcissistic personality disorder has been referred to treatment because she vandalised the car of one of her work colleagues: 'He smiled at me in the morning and I waited all day for him to ask me out and he didn't. No one gets away with rejecting and abusing me in this way. He deserved it.'

Contemplation

In this stage the client realises there are personal problems. He/she starts thinking about possible ways to get rid of the problems but has not yet made the decision to change.

The main worry in this stage is the fear of losing something pleasant and the fear of not being able to solve the problems adequately. The person's mind works like an old-fashioned weighing scale. On the one side there are arguments for change and on the other there are arguments favouring no change.

Obstacles that prevent progress from contemplation to determination are:

- A lack of concern about the problems (knowing that something is not ok does not automatically lead to concern over these facts).
- A fear that the pleasurable aspects of the present status quo will diminish and that no other positives will be returned.
- Fear of not being able to change (lack of competence).

So in order to be able to make a decision as to whether personal change is needed, we need to know that we are involved in the problem, we need to be concerned about that, we need to see ourselves as worthwhile and see ourselves as competent enough to resolve the problems.

Meet some contemplators

- John states after a few sessions of motivation focused CBT: 'This drinking gets me into trouble; I will lose my licence this time for certain. But giving up hanging out with my mates and getting completely plastered – not so sure about that.'
- Belinda can see a different perspective after a few sessions: 'Vandalising someone's car after they have hurt your feelings – perhaps I am a bit too self-centred and sensitive but you can't let people get away with treating you like a doormat!'

Determination/decision

This is the transition from contemplation to active change. It is also possible to decide not to change, dropping out of the circle of change by way of exit 1. The main obstacle that will prevent clients from reaching a decision is a lack of knowledge regarding change methods, that is not being aware of a change method that fit their preferences.

This is the crux of motivational interviewing: getting the client involved in wise decision-making. Too often we make decisions based on our beliefs and not on the available facts. Knowing the facts is not enough; we have to apply the facts to ourselves as well. Facts are known (I don't take any leisure/relaxation time) but the person cannot see how this behaviour links with problem issues (being very tired all the time).

Developing motivation for change is a decision-making process whereby the person needs to learn to be objective about all the issues and accept the facts as they are presented. On a personal level one can see how challenging this is. Accepting that one has been engaging in self- or other-damaging behaviours for years is not an easy task and it might be easier to just distort the information ('It is not that bad'). It also involves being able to assess one's personal strengths objectively. Sometimes people have 'forgotten' or distorted previous experiences of competence and endurance ('That was just luck').

Active change

In this stage people alter their overt behaviour and this is where traditional change-directed psychological therapy comes in with all its strategies.

Maintenance

The client tries to stabilise the changes he or she has made. He or she tries to prevent a relapse into the old unwanted behaviour (for instance drinking too much alcohol). Clients may seek professional help in this stage too because they are afraid of a relapse. Clients may remain in this stage for up to six months. However, if preoccupation with a possible relapse vanishes and the client doesn't identify him or herself any longer with the former problems, he or she 'steps out' of the circle of change by way of the permanent exit.

Relapse

Relapsing means returning to the old problematic ways of doing life. A relapse mostly results in going back to the stage of contemplation. Clients will become increasingly sceptical about the possibilities of change after experiencing relapses.

In summary

Motivation for change consists of five elements:

1　The client needs to be aware of the fact that their behaviour has an impact on the problematic situation they find themselves in (knowledge).
2　The client needs to have sufficient self-appreciation (or using a different word, self-esteem) to see themselves as worthwhile enough to be without the problems (self-worth).
3　The client needs to be concerned about the problems they experience (concern).

4   The client needs to have some confidence in their own ability to bring about change (felt competence).
5   The client needs to know about change methods that they believe can work for them (trust in the change process).

Trust in the process

A bit more about the last point above: in order to really make the necessary steps towards change the client needs to believe in the change methods that are offered. The felt competence is about the client's self-perception, while this element is about the change methods that are on offer. Clients may believe that they will be able to change, but they lose faith when informed about the change methods available. (For example, the message 'The only way to overcome your personality problem is by going for three years into a therapeutic community' might have a discouraging effect on some clients.)

Decision making

Becoming motivated for change is a decision-making process whereby all of the five above-mentioned elements are processed. In many of life's decisions we process these in an implicit manner, often without really being aware of the process. As a result of this we often make decisions that are only based on part of the complete picture:

- Dedicated smokers seldom think of all the consequences of their habit before lighting up.
- When buying that dream house and signing the loan paperwork, we may 'forget' certain financial obligations that would have put our loan application in jeopardy.
- When declining to board a plane because we are terrified of flying, we forget the statistics (flying is safer then driving) and our own competence (in the past we have flown successfully).

In a therapeutic context, we have to make this process explicit (and bring elements to the foreground that the client finds difficult to acknowledge).

Cognitive Dissonance

The end result of a successful motivation enhancement process is 'cognitive dissonance' (Festinger et al., 1956; Festinger, 1957). A state of cognitive dissonance is experienced as unpleasant by clients and therefore most people try to avoid it or once in it try to escape from it. *Cognitive dissonance* is an uncomfortable feeling caused by holding two contradictory ideas simultaneously. The theory of cognitive dissonance proposes that people have a motivational drive to reduce dissonance (because if feels unpleasant) by changing one or more of the following: attitudes, beliefs and behaviours. Dissonance occurs when people perceive a logical inconsistency in their beliefs, when one idea implies the opposite of another. The emotional consequence of the dissonance might be guilt, anger, frustration, or embarrassment.

Examples of opposing ideas in practice are:

- I am a healthy person/My drinking has cause irreparable damage.
- I am a very important person/People are treating me as just anyone.
- I am an honest person/I have told lies and stolen to cover up personal mistakes.

Ways to resolve cognitive dissonance are:

- Behaviour change: stop drinking; stop being dishonest.
- Attitudinal change: being healthy is widely overrated, let's have fun; what other people think is unimportant; I am not honest.

A very elegant example of changing preferences as a result of challenging circumstances is told in the fable 'The Fox and the Grapes' by Aesop (ca. 620–564 BCE), where the fox decides that the grapes he is unable to reach are probably not ripe enough to eat anyway: desiring something, then criticising it because it proves unattainable. We see this phenomenon in clinical practice often, when a client embarks on a change process that proves more difficult then envisaged: 'This therapy is not for me, all the problems were exaggerated anyway, no real need to change.'

It is clear that in practice the aim would be to promote behaviour change in the healthy direction: stopping drinking, behaving more honestly and/or developing more realistic attitudes: I am just as important as everyone else and don't deserve special treatment.

Engagement strategies

Let's go back for a moment to the characteristics that are typical for people with personality difficulties: rigid and inflexible patterns of behaviour and thinking; negative consequences of behaviour are often ignored; and the 'instinctive' reaction is that improvement can come through the change of others. This means that the psychological therapist who works with clients with personality difficulties has to be prepared to apply specific strategies to get these clients ready for therapy, ready for change and motivated to work towards change. It sometimes feels a bit like trying to sell something to people who do not want to buy anything!

We suggest that there is a distinct set of techniques that can be used to this effect: motivational interviewing (Denissen and van Bilsen, 1987; van Bilsen, 1985a, 1986a, 1991, 1995a; van Bilsen and van Emst, 1989; van Bilsen and Wilke, 1998).

Motivational Interviewing (MI)

MI is a set of techniques of talking to people about difficult topics without alienating them. Therapists working with personality disorders are after all often talking to people who do not want to change and who might feel quite antagonistic against the therapist and everything he/she represents. So the first port of call is to talk to clients without increasing their antagonism.

Motivation for change is based on knowledge, concern, self-appreciation, felt competence and trust in the change process. MI makes these elements of motivation a target and is exclusively focused on enhancing these within the client. In other words MI is specifically focused on creating cognitive dissonance:

- I am a worthwhile person and I am destroying this person.
- I am concerned about my situation and could change it for the better if I wanted to.

Traditionally (Miller and Rollnick, 2002; Hettema et al., 2004) the perspective was that in order to motivate people the best strategies were to tell people what to think and do and to threaten people with negative consequences.

Unfortunately these traditional motivational strategies only seem to work in a very limited way and then only with people who are ready to change (e.g. are in the stage of *action*). These strategies trigger resistance and opposition in clients in other stages. Imposing insight on people will result in them starting a debate; giving people knowledge will result in that knowledge being disputed; try to teach skills to people in the stage of contemplation and you will have very reluctant participants.

Key Assumptions of MI

The first assumption is that motivation is the end product of a complex interaction between person/client elements and environmental influences. This means that motivation is not something that grows within clients without any connection to what happens around them. Motivation to change fluctuates as a result of a person's experiences with life, with other people and how things go for them in general. Let's be honest: would you, the reader, be motivated to change if you were in a very problematic situation but were convinced that you could only make things worse? If you know that your experience is that whenever you try to improve things they fail, then you are bound to be very sceptical of new attempts.

The second assumption is that motivation is interpersonal: motivation for change is influenced by interpersonal relationships and interactions. Specific interactions in specific situations can make us deny and lie. Take for example that you are discussing your tax return with the tax office and you notice that you claimed as an expense a workshop on MI that you had been compensated for by your employer. The taxman asks whether you indeed were compensated for this from your employer. You know that if you say yes, that in all likelihood he will scrutinise your whole tax file with a lot more care and may find other inconsistencies. If you say that you did not receive any compensation it will be highly unlikely that he will find out you lied and the whole inspection will be over in five minutes. It would take an extremely moral person to admit the mistake and suffer the consequences in a situation like this. Most people try to avoid 'punishment' in interpersonal situations. As a consequence of this we also have to admit that resistance to change is interpersonal. Our lies we told the taxman are a form of resistance. This was triggered by the specific circumstances. With clients the specific circumstances are that they can discover that there is a serious problem and that they may have to bring about some change. People are inclined to protect themselves from potential bad news: if it seems the therapist could bring bad news, the client will go in defensive/denial mode.

The third assumption is that our behaviours as therapists matter: what we do is important. This follows logically from the first two assumptions, but is important to reiterate, as many clinicians seem to forget this. Too often we hear clinicians state that they just want the best for their clients when they have been trying to convince clients of their problems and are stunned by the clients' denial of problems that are very obvious to everyone else. Good intentions are the basic standard but they need to be translated in clinician behaviours that promote motivation for change. Lecturing, explaining and arguing do not produce motivated clients; they will produce clients who are very well versed in debating with therapists why they should not change. This is especially so for clients with personality problems. These clients have often been engaging in extreme self-defeating behaviour that has resulted in many hospital admissions, serious medical problems and sometimes incarceration in prisons or forensic institutions. Many clinicians tell us: 'I just wanted them to know how self-defeating their behaviours are.' Persuasion is usually not an effective method to increase motivation and change, as it leads to counterarguments, especially if agreeing with the other person would mean accepting something that is perceived to be unpleasant.

MI: how it all works

We would like to address this in three steps. First, we will review the spirit of MI, followed by the basic principles of MI (Miller and Rollnick, 2002) and finally we will review what we see as the main MI techniques (Miller and Rollnick, 2002; van Bilsen, 1986b). We want to stress here that MI is not merely a set of techniques. Just applying it like a set of techniques is like playing a beautiful piece of music by playing each note to perfection but forgetting the whole. It will sound like music, but its beauty will be vastly reduced.

Applying MI works similarly: applying the techniques described needs to be based on understanding the spirit and principles of MI.

MI Spirit

MI is based on *acceptance* instead of demands. In working with complex clients with long-standing problems psychological therapy services often impose demands upon the clients that counteract the development of motivation for change (remember demands create resistance). Examples of these demands are: stop drinking alcohol, stop self-harming, stop stealing and stop lying. The most creative demand we are aware of being imposed on clients is in a family therapy service in the Netherlands. Here families are only taken into therapy when they have stopped having arguments for two weeks. We are sure you all know of similar demands in the addiction services or in working with clients with personality difficulties. MI is accepting what is, instead of demanding what should be.

In line with one of the corner stones of CBT, motivational interviewing focuses on *collaboration* instead of confrontation. This makes MI a de facto Socratic process in the extreme. The building blocks of motivation are not imposed upon the client, but are jointly discovered by client and therapist in what on the surface looks like a casual chat, but what in actual fact is a detailed and specific way of talking to clients.

Education is one of the core strategies in CBT. When doing motivational work, it is important to restrain this. MI focuses much more on *evocation*. In evocation the clinician focuses on eliciting issues from the client that are going to be the focus of the discussions. This is opposed to education whereby the clinician imparts his/her wisdom on the client. There is of course a need for educational activities in CBT, but to apply education within a motivation enhancement strategy is often self-defeating. Giving the client space to talk and by using specific MI techniques focusing, that conversation will be much more helpful.

Basic MI Principles

Develop discrepancy

MI is focused on developing a discrepancy between where clients are now and where they would like to be. For this, two things are needed. First of all clients need to develop a clear and objective perspective of where they are now. In working with clients with personality difficulties many clinicians are so impressed by the problems and suffering of their clients that they move immediately to goal setting, without having investigated the current circumstances of the client in clear and objective detail. In these situations we often see clients making some haphazard attempts at changing but with the first challenge go back to the status quo. This is possible because the therapist has not allowed the negative aspects of the status quo to come to the foreground. Hence the client can easily believe that avoiding the difficulty of the change process will result in going back to a less problematic status quo. The second element of this is of course 'hope and vision'. The therapist has to assist the client to develop a vision of a less problematic future and instil hope in the client that this future is attainable.

Roll with Resistance

Resistance can be defined as disagreeing with the therapist ('I don't need any time for myself, hard work is the best way to overcome problems') or denying obvious facts ('Hard work always improves my mood' when from the data collection by the client it is clear that she feels more and more depressed after hard work). In a traditional approach the therapist may try to convince clients of the therapist's perspective. Within an MI approach the strategy is to 'roll with the resistance' by asking clients to explain their perspective a bit more. This is based on martial arts principles. If you want to create movement it is pointless if you do the same thing as your opponent. When both push or pull at the same time, there will be a standstill and a battle of strength. However, when one pulls and the other reacts by pushing, there is movement and movement opens up the potential for change.

Express Empathy

Developing motivation for change can be a painful process for the client. It is a journey of discovery where what is unearthed may be negative and unpleasant. In order for the client to be able to tolerate this, the therapist needs to be very empathic and respectful of clients' emotional responses to the process. Expressing empathy is bringing across to the client that we understand their perspective; we understand their pain and discomfort. Please note that just saying to the client: 'I know how you feel' is bound to backfire as, in all honesty, we don't *know* how the client feels; we can only attempt to reflect back to the client how we understand they are feeling and how we understand their thinking.

Support Self-efficacy

MI is focused on clients' self-efficacy and self-determination. Often clients with long-standing and enduring problems such as personality difficulties will enter a psychological therapy situation with statements such as: 'I have to be here', 'They make me come and talk to you', 'I have no choice'. It is important for the clinician to create an atmosphere of choice and self-determination, by focusing on choices the client has.

Table 7.1

Client	Possible self-efficacy reactions
I have to be here	• So you have to be here – how did you make the decision to go along with that demand?
	• So you have to be here – how would you like to make use of the time we have?
They make me come and talk to you	• They make you come and talk to me – have you decided what you want to talk about?
I have no choice	• You feel you don't have a choice – how did you come to that conclusion?

Techniques of MI

We differentiate between basic MI techniques (selective active listening and fine-tuned reflections) and advanced MI techniques (positive restructuring and provocative techniques).

Selective Active Listening

Selective active listening consists of three components: active listening, selection of motivational elements and asking motivational questions.

Active listening

Active listening means that we are tuned in to what clients are telling us. We are focused on 'getting' what they are trying to convey. We use non-verbal signals of eye-contact, nodding and hmm-hmm-ing to convey we are interested. We use repetitions, reflections and summaries to feed back to clients how we have understood their stories. In MI the clinician tries to do this in a way that invites the client to expand on what they have said. Often a reflection or summary is ended with a question like 'Could you tell me a bit more about that?'

Selection of motivational elements

This active listening is not a 'blind' activity. Not everything the client says is treated equally. Signs of the building blocks of motivation (knowledge, concern, self-appreciation, felt competence and trust in the change process) are given more attention in the repetitions, reflections and the summaries of the therapist. This works as reinforcement of desirable behaviour (for most people a therapist focusing on issues that they have just talked about themselves is perceived as something positive) and what is reinforced is likely to occur more frequently. If this reinforcement is combined with an invitation to talk more about these issues, we have a very strong combination: motivational talk by the client is reinforced. This is followed by an invitation to expand on this topic. The result is *more* motivational talk. The consequence of this should not be underestimated. We know that the best way to convince ourselves is to hear ourselves talk. So the more we get the client to talk motivational talk, the more we increase the client's belief in what he/she is saying.

Asking motivational questions

Motivational questions are questions focused on getting the client to talk about any of the five motivational building blocks. For example: 'You mentioned your tiredness. Could you tell me a bit more about the problems this tiredness causes for you' (eliciting factual problem information); or 'You mentioned your tiredness – how do you feel about being tired all the time?' (eliciting concern).

Fine-tuned Reflections

Selective active listening is the foundation technique of motivational interviewing; without this base all other interventions will fall flat. Fine-tuned reflections are a set of techniques that look and sound like reflections and to all ends and purposes they are presented to the client as reflections, but their intent and effect is often not the same as with a standard reflection.

Feeling reflection

A feeling reflection can be used when the therapist senses a strong feeling behind the spoken words of clients. The therapist can then reflect the feeling in a low-key manner, leaving it with clients to 'accept' or 'reject' the educated guess of the therapist. If the therapist gets it wrong, e.g. the client rejects the feeling interpretation of the therapist, then it is vital to accept this rejection and not 'push' the client in accepting that they were feeling angry or anxious. The impact of carefully presented feeling reflections is a deepening of the therapeutic rapport between therapist and client.

Conflict reflection

Conflict reflections are used when the therapist notices ambiguity in the client. Sceptical clients may be in two minds about certain issues: 'On the one hand I really would like to get rid of this tiredness but I certainly don't have a mental illness' or 'I don't want to end up like my friend Bob, who was killed in a car crash, but I really like getting completely wasted with my mates'. It is a bit like an approach-approach or an avoidance-avoidance conflict. In MI it is important to feed these internal conflicts back to the client but *finish with the side promoting change*, followed by an invitation to expand. What happens will be that clients will expand on the element that promotes change, as this was the last element before the question to expand.

Table 7.2

Client	Therapist	Client's response
I am so depressed, it is all awful.	If I understand you correctly, you are in the deepest pit of depression 24 hours per day, there is not one second when things are less black.	Well, it is not as bad as that, when I walk the dog …
I can't help that I am in prison. I didn't make myself kill my parents. If they just had given me the money there would have been no problems.	If I understand you correctly you are saying that you are completely powerless, you are a pawn in the game of life with no influence over your fate whatsoever?	I wouldn't say I was completely powerless …

Overshooting and undershooting reflections

Overshooting and undershooting are used when clients seem to have rigid beliefs that go against motivation for change. The aim of these reflections is for the client to *disagree* with the therapist. What the therapist does is to feed back to the client in the style of a reflection but with an exaggerated or minimised version of what the client has just told the therapist. The presentation style of the therapist needs to be very empathic, hesitant, trying to really understand the client. Some examples are shown in Table 7.2.

These 'shooting' reflections are followed up by 'normal' reflective listening. The response of the client to the 'shooting' is often in the direction of motivation. In the first example in Table 7.2 the client adds that there are moments that are better than others and in the second example the client takes back some self-efficacy.

Overshooting and undershooting need to be presented with empathy otherwise they soon sound sarcastic and critical.

Positive restructuring

This is the first of the advanced strategies. Positive restructuring is based on the premise that apart from people with a psychopathic personality disorder, humans are well meaning and have good intentions. People's behaviour may have a negative impact but the intent is in general positive. Therapists enhance clients' self-esteem by focusing attention on client's positive intentions. This is *not* praise, but goes beyond the words and deeds: it focuses on the intention. For example:

- A client who has been trying to change for many years, who has tried many therapists and now wants to give it another shot with this therapist: You are a very persistent person.
- A client who arrives at the office in a desperate state, who has been told that her three children will be taken into care unless she demonstrates some radical change: You want the best for your children.

It is often much easier to focus on negative intentions. In the first example we could easily say that the client lacks any willpower and is not able to tolerate discomfort. In the second example we could have said that the mother has been neglecting her maternal duties because of her gambling addiction. However, would that have influenced motivation for change?

Provocative techniques

Provocative techniques should only be used when nothing else works. There are different kinds of provocations. There is the 'Columbo technique' whereby the therapists display clumsiness and relative incompetence. This can be used in situations where the therapist has a captive audience (the client *has* to meet with the therapist) and whereby the client feels very threatened by the supposed competence and superiority of the therapist. By becoming clumsy and slightly incompetent, therapists reduce their standing and as a result make clients more comfortable. Another provocative technique is the 'devil's advocate' technique. This can be particularly well used in situations whereby clients find it difficult to reach a decision, for instance to start with therapy or not. Therapists then subtly start to advocate for the side of lacking motivation/not wanting to change *and presents that in a slightly negative light*. For instance, a client who finds it very difficult to decide whether to embark on an anger-management programme to curb his aggressive and self-destructive outbursts could be told: 'Well, entering a therapy programme like this is not easy. Many people don't have the will power and character strength to bring it to a good end and it would be such a shame if you would be disappointed in yourself. Why would you want to risk that?'

Reflections on engagement strategies

MI is not a panacea for all sceptical and unmotivated clients. It is a tool to assist clinicians to talk to sceptical clients without getting into unproductive arguments and it is furthermore a set of techniques aimed at gradually building motivation for change.

MI is proposed as an engagement strategy for sceptical clients. Many clients with a diagnosis of personality disorder who are referred for psychological therapy may fall into the sceptical category. The model we can use to assess the level of their scepticism is the stages of change model. This will provide a road map for the motivation enhancement work that needs to be done. Specific and detailed motivational interventions are described; however, it is once again important to outline that they are no panacea for all challenging clients.

AN EXAMPLE OF MOTIVATIONAL INTERVIEWING

This is an excerpt of a third session with Belinda. Belinda worked as a PA to a CEO of a large company. She was also seen by a psychiatrist who diagnosed her with narcissistic personality disorder. She had been referred because of her unprovoked aggressive outburst towards colleagues at work. Her outstanding skills as a PA had protected her from criminal charges. Belinda has expressed during previous sessions that she is just attending these meetings to keep everyone happy. She does not see that there is any problem.

Table 7.3

Who talks	Verbatim	Comments
T	Welcome back. What would you like to put on the agenda today?	
B	That question again – aren't you supposed to be the specialist here?	Attack on the structure of CBT.
T	Yes, that question again – you are so right. Which items would you like to put on the agenda today?	Persistence.
B	Well, you said I could put anything on the agenda, anything at all – it did not need to be connected to what I did to Bob's car.	She had damaged Bob's car when she thought he was insulting her. Bob is a colleague.
T	You are right again – this is your time and you can add things to the agenda that you want to talk about.	Confirmation of client's contribution.
B	Well it is nothing really, but I thought that Felicity was really behaving strangely to me. Perhaps it is better not to talk about that. Aren't you going to suggest what to talk about?	
T	So there was something in the way Felicity behaved towards you, but not really worth mentioning …	Reflection and mild undershooting.
B	It wasn't nothing you know – she really snubbed me and made me look a fool.	
T	… made you look a fool. Do you want to put that on the agenda today?	
B	Ok then.	
T	So that is one thing for today's agenda – anything else?	
B	No, that's all – for the rest everything is just fine.	
T	So, correct me if I am wrong – apart from the issue with Felicity, everything else in your life is 100% ok and perfect?	Overshooting.
B	Well, no not perfect – it would be nice to be appreciated more and not have to take a lot of negativity from other people.	
T	… it would be nice to be appreciated and not have to take a lot of negativity from other people – would that be something for today's agenda as well?	Reflection and invitation to put issues on the agenda.

(Continued)

Table 7.3 (Continued)

Who talks	Verbatim	Comments
B	We might as well.	
T	So we have three things that you would like on the agenda today: what happened with Felicity, not having to take a lot of negativity from other people and that it would be nice to be appreciated. Anything you would like to add to that?	
B	No that sounds like enough.	
T	Which of these three items would you like to start with?	
B	Not being appreciated.	
T	Not being appreciated – can you tell me a bit more about that?	Open question.
B	Well that I am sitting here is evidence of that isn't it? I work very hard at making things run smoothly, I arrive early, take work home and it all does run smoothly and then they treat me like this!	
T	From what I understand, you really want to do things well at work – you give it more than 100%!	Positive restructuring.
B	Yes [*tearful now*], I try to do my best and then for such a small mistake I am sent to a psychologist and a psychiatrist. It is just not fair.	
T	Let me see if I get this right. On the one hand, we have Belinda working very hard and competently at running the office and on the other hand we have Belinda causing £5000 damage to Bob's car. What you are saying is that they just should have accepted the damage as one of those small things and it should be forgotten?	Provocative reflection.
B	If you say it like that, it is of course not a small thing. But I am paying for the damage and this is not the first time I have been treated like this. There was the problem with Sally. I had to pay for her computer because I poured water over it.	
T	So you had to pay for the damage you did to Bob's car, you had to pay for Sally's computer … do you want to continue to go through life and pay for damage you do other folks' property?	Question to elicit self-motivational statements.
B	No of course not! I want to be happy, but it seems like everyone else is focused on making me unhappy.	
T	If I understand you correctly, you are saying you want to be happy, you deserve to be happy but many things happen that cause you unhappiness.	Reflection.
B	Yes [*tearful*] and it doesn't stop, this week this thing with Felicity. She is one of the associate directors and I have helped her with a number of presentations she had to do, making the Powerpoints look all glitzy and nice. Yesterday I was juggling ten things at the same time and I was on the phone to the States about the next conference. She comes into the office and asks whether Allan and Tracy want to go for some lunch. She did not ask me. This is so humiliating, this is so unfair.	

(Continued)

Table 7.3 *(Continued)*

Who talks	Verbatim	Comments
T	It seems that other people have the power to cause you to feel really bad. A while ago Bob made you feel really angry and now Tracy makes you feel humiliated. Would you be interested in learning to reduce the power other people have over you?	Question focused on eliciting self-motivational statements.
B	That would be nice, but I really don't see that that is possible. I have always been like this, this sensitive.	
T	You have always been very sensitive and you think this is something very difficult to change although you would like to be less overwhelmed by these negative feelings.	Paraphrase, finish with motivation last.
B	Yes, if only I knew what to do.	
T	Well, you started today by saying that I was the specialist and I am. If you are interested in learning to give other people less power over your emotions, I can help you achieve that. In order to do that properly, I would need to ask you a lot of questions and I am not sure whether you could be bothered to answer them. It could be a bit tedious.	Summary with a provocative tail.
B	Well, if it can save me in the future from paying for new computers and car repairs, let's go for it!	

Understanding check

Things you should be able to do after reading this chapter:

1 Describe the stages of change model.
2 Describe the building block for motivation for change.
3 Give an outline of the spirit and fundamentals of motivational interviewing.
4 Give some examples of overshooting, positive restructuring and conflict reflections.

8

REFLECTION ON CBT AS A PSYCHOLOGICAL THERAPY FOR PERSONALITY DISORDERS

In this chapter you will learn about:

- The evidence supporting psychological treatments for personality problems.
- Guidelines for building evidence-based intervention plans for personality problems.

Introduction

The evidence base for the effectiveness of CBT in the treatment for personality disorders is limited and varies strongly from one personality disorder diagnosis to the next. Are we trying to do the impossible? Are we using 'software' (= psychological therapies) to correct 'hardware' (= structural personality defects)? The number of forensic psychiatry beds in the UK is rising; are we medicalising and psychologising badness? This trend of medicalising and psychologising badness can be seen from early days onwards as Foucault (1988) states. The trend can perhaps best be observed in how western 'civilisation' deals with the issue of alcohol and drug use. Drugs that were mainly associated with white people (alcohol and tobacco) are seen as ok to use and tax (apart from the brief prohibition period between 1920 and 1933 in the USA), while drugs (heroin and cocaine) that were originally mainly associated with Chinese immigrants in the US and black people were demonised (van Bilsen, 1986b). To be able to call someone a deviant who suffers from a psychiatric problem (a personality disorder no less) will disempower and annul everything they say (Conrad, 1992). From this perspective we strongly recommend to clinicians working with personality disorders to always keep an open mind to what clients have to say and beware of the power of labelling.

Prevalence and Cost

Researchers found that the prevalence for any personality disorder in the United States is 9.1 per cent. Specific prevalence rates for borderline personality disorder and antisocial personality disorder were estimated at 1.4 per cent and 0.6 per cent, respectively (Lenzenweger et al, 2007). These data are similar to UK data where Cold et al. (2006) found around 10 per cent of their sample to qualify for a DSM-IV diagnosis of personality disorder.

People with personality difficulties are costly to the health service. Borderline personality disorder imposes a significant burden on primary and secondary health care services as well as other statutory service providers. Some studies have attempted to calculate the potential cost impact of personality disorders more generally. In a cost of illness study, Smith et al. (1995) estimated that the annual cost of personality disorders to the National Health Service (NHS) amounted to over £61 million in 1986. Rendu et al. (2002) assessed the costs of personality disorders amongst patients attending general practices in the UK. The mean total costs (health and non-health related) for patients with personality disorder are almost double that of those without personality disorder. This study also highlighted the considerable burden on non-health care providers and the wider economy. The total economic impact of personality disorders remains largely unknown (Palmer et al., 2006).

This all makes it very important to use effective and evidence-based interventions in the treatment of people with personality difficulties. It also makes it important to be aware of the limitations of psychological interventions. Let us take you through a comparison. Let us assume that a 32-year-old man has lost his eyesight in a car accident. How long would you be prepared to continue investing in medical treatment to help restore his eyesight? Would you be willing to invest in making the young man's environment suitable for a life as full as possible without eyesight? This is in fact what we constantly have to think about when working with clients with severe and long-standing problems such as personality disorders: do we aim for cure or do we aim for care? How long will we try to cure before we switch to care?

One of the great and charismatic clinicians and researchers in the field of personality disorders is undoubtedly Marsha Linehan. In one of her workshops she compares working with personality disorders with flying a plane into a busy airport. Sometimes you have to wait for a while before you can have your landing slot, but when you get your landing slot, it is all systems go! With clients who have personality problems, we may have to offer them care (e.g. support them so they don't harm themselves and/or others) while they are not yet motivated or willing to change. When the moment of motivation arrives, we should be ready to offer evidence-based therapy. Like trying to land a plane at a busy airport when you don't have a landing slot, offering 'cure'-focused therapy to unmotivated clients will lead to disaster.

Evidence base

Reviewing the evidence base for the treatment of personality disorder is a disappointing experience. The Dutch Institute for the Development of clinical

Guidelines (Trimbos Instituut) published multidisciplinary guidelines for the treatment of people with a diagnosis of personality disorders. Their general recommendations (Landelijke Stuurgroep Multidisciplinaire Richtlijnontwikkeling in de GGZ, 2008) are as follows (Winston et al., 1991, 1994; Piper et al., 1998, 1999; Perry et al., 1999; Svartberg et al., 2004):

- Individual psychological therapies based on various theoretical frameworks (for instance CBT or psychodynamic psychotherapy) are helpful interventions in reducing symptoms and personality pathology and improvement of social functioning for people with a range of personality problems.
- Effectiveness of CBT does *not* differ from effectiveness of psychodynamic psychotherapy for a variety of personality difficulties.
- Supportive psychodynamic psychotherapy results in lower drop-out rates than more expressive or confrontational forms of psychotherapy.

This all sounds reasonably positive, until you realise that this is as good as it gets for personality disorders in general. The terms CBT and psychodynamic psychotherapy are broad. Both are very big trees with many branches; does it mean that all CBT and all psychodynamic psychotherapy is effective?

The guidelines give more specific guidance of borderline personality disorders. There is *evidence* that dialectical behaviour therapy is an effective treatment leading to a reduction in crisis admissions, reduction of symptoms of self-harm, suicidality and high-risk behaviours and an improvement of social functioning. There are *indications* that the *family members module* of dialectical behaviour therapy results in a reduction of the burden to family members. It is *plausible* that *schema-focused therapy* is effective in the reduction of symptoms and personality pathology and an improvement in social functioning and that schema-focused therapy is more effective then transference-focused psychotherapy. It is furthermore *plausible* that treatments based on an *interpersonal* and *psychodynamic* modality result in a reduction of symptoms, health care consumption and personality pathology. There are indications that cognitive analytic therapy, cognitive therapy and transference-focused psychotherapy are all effective in the reduction of symptoms and personality pathology and an improvement in social functioning (Meares et al., 1999; Ryle et al., 2000; Clarkin et al., 2001; Hoffman et al., 2005; Brown et al., 2004; McQuillan et al., 2005; Nordahl and Nysaeter, 2005; Stevenson and Meares, 1992).

Bateman and Tyrer (2004) postulate that in order to demonstrate effectiveness, a treatment for personality disordered clients would need to:

1 Demonstrate efficacy in randomised controlled trials over control *treatments* when used for a pure form of the personality disorder.
2 Demonstrate similar outcomes in pragmatic randomised controlled trials.
3 Show consistency in efficacy across settings when used with appropriate treatment fidelity.
4 Maintain outcomes over time (preferably more than one year).

They conclude that there are no treatments that have passed this test. There has been more charisma than 'real' evidence in discussions about CBT-based treatments for personality disorders. Charismatic presenters and authors (Padesky, 1990; Linehan, 1993; Young, Klosko and Weishaar, 2003) have infected many clinicians with their enthusiasm. However, this enthusiasm is not matched with hard evidence of the kind Bateman and Tyrer (2004) suggest is needed.

A large number of studies have been carried out, which suggest that various treatments may have a positive impact on people with a diagnosis of personality disorders on a range of outcome measures (Warren et al., 2003). However, weaknesses in the methodology of the majority of these studies mean that the quality of the evidence for the treatment of personality disorders is poor. Regarding people with severe problems and a diagnosis of personality disorder, requiring residential treatment or incarceration, there is some evidence for the effectiveness of cognitive behavioural therapy at lower levels of security, where a number of randomised control trials have been carried out. Until similar studies have been carried out among populations known to be severely personality disordered, these results cannot be assumed to apply to this group. Dialectical behavioural therapy (DBT) is a variation of cognitive behavioural therapy, which is aimed at changing the typical behaviour patterns of individuals with borderline personality disorder, such as suicidal tendencies. There is some evidence of the short-term effectiveness of DBT among women, although this comes primarily from outpatient settings (Warren et al., 2003). There is further evidence that both psychodynamic therapy and CBT are effective in the treatment of personality disorders (Leichsenring and Leibing, 2003) but the number of studies is limited so this is a preliminary conclusion.

More recently there have been replications and additional studies investigating the efficacy of dialectical behaviour therapy for borderline personality disorders (Linehan, 1993; Verheul et al., 2003), problem-solving therapy and psychoeducation (Huband et al., 2007), and schema-focused therapy for borderline personality disorder (Giesen-Bloo et al., 2006). These are all well-controlled studies indicating the effectiveness of the interventions involved; however, the main problem with these studies remains and that is of small sample sizes, combined with multi-faceted treatment interventions, relatively short follow-up and by definition a heterogeneous group of clients. What works when for whom and for how long remains a mystery.

The answer for now may be with Bateman and Fonagy's (2000) suggestions. After reviewing the literature they suggest a range of generic (read a-theoretical) guidelines. Treatment should be:

1 Well structured.
2 Devote considerable effort to enhancing compliance.
3 Clear in focus (focused on problems and goals).
4 Theoretically coherent to both therapist and client.

5 Relatively long term.
6 Invested in the therapeutic relationship.
7 Well integrated with other services available.

We would like to add one criterion to this: meaningful outcomes. Too often results of treatments have a statistical significance but lack real-life meaning. For example, a statistical significant difference of three points on a problem severity scale is interesting, but may not be that meaningful in real life. In other words, reducing self-harm behaviour from 40 times per month to 27 times may be statistically significant, but does it have a real meaning?

Bateman and Tyrer (2004) are carefully optimistic about the efficacy of psychological treatments for people with a personality disorder: 'Psychotherapeutic interventions show promise, although interpretation of the literature is problematic: the number of patients in most trials is small, outcome measures are questionable, follow-up is limited and treatments are multifaceted, complex interventions in which the effective components are unclear.' In other words, we know that something seems to do some good sometimes, but how much good, when and for whom and with what is undecided.

Treating disorders, personalities or people experiencing problems

Could it be that we are trying to do too much? All the treatments described focus on the 'disorder of personality'. Agreed, they have specific measures focusing on beliefs, cognitions, feelings and behaviours, but by definition a treatment for personality disorders focuses on treating the personality disorder exactly,. Most research also tries to demonstrate the effectiveness of treatment by using indicators such as suicide attempts and hospital admissions. This is a strange habit if you come to think of it. If medical doctors would do this, we could see interesting discussions. Let's say we have a rugby player, Theo, who has been injured. If his injury is not fixed he will not be able to play rugby; if the doctor can fix him he can continue to play rugby. Rugby players stand a very strong chance of injury (Gabbett and Hodgson, 2003). During every match there is an average of ten injuries and during each training session three. This would mean that a successful intervention of a doctor to fix Theo's problem would result in Theo *costing* the health system more as he would go back to rugby and get injured more often. If the injury is dealt with unsuccessfully he would take up working out in the local gym, which has a much lower incidence rate of injuries: treatment failure would be cheaper. In our drive to prove the value of psychological therapy, we sometimes forget that psychological therapy is not a miracle cure and it certainly is not a fix for society's many ailments. A psychological therapy is in essence two people collaborating to achieve personal change in feelings, behaviour and thinking of one person, a change that is based on self-identified problems and goals. We have never come across a goal such as: 'I would like to cost the taxpayer less money as a result of this treatment.'

It is also interesting that most interventions are multi-faceted. A good example of this is dialectical behaviour therapy (DBT), which consists of a treatment structure, individual therapy and skills training groups (Linehan et al, 1999). Treatments labelled as DBT have produced promising results; however, what these studies do not inform us about is how much of the multi-faceted therapy is needed to produce a meaningful result. Is it necessary for clients to take part and complete *all* ingredients or can clients make a selection?

The scientist-practitioner that each self-respecting cognitive behaviour therapist is, searches in vain for the definitive piece of research indicating that beyond reasonable doubt *this* form of CBT is most effective for personality disorders.

Individualised formulations

Perhaps it is time to go back to basics and follow on from what we suggested earlier: treatments need to be based on individualised formulations of problems and goals, with a detailed analysis of mechanisms that prevented goal attainment so far. The mechanisms that prevented goal attainment then need to become the focus of therapeutic attention. In other words, instead of investigating whether interventions work for personality disorders, it might be wiser to evaluate if interventions reduce identified problems and improve goal attainment.

Based on the available research findings we can identify a range of cognitive behavioural interventions that were components of treatments that have received support:

1 Cognitive restructuring (Linehan, 1993; Davidson and Tyrer, 1996; Young, Klosko and Weishaar, 2003; Giesen-Bloo et al., 2006) focuses on the transdiagnostic processes of attentional bias, reasoning problems and maladaptive behavioural processes. In many studies this core technique of CBT has been demonstrated to be able to help clients change their behaviours, change the way they feel and develop more rational thinking processes.
2 Problem-solving skills training (Linehan, 1993; Verheul, 2003) focuses on the transdiagnostic processes of attentional, bias memory, bias, biased thought processes and maladaptive behavioural processes. Training people in problem solving skills has been demonstrated to achieve that people overcome problem solving deficits and improve the quality of their problem solving (D'Zurilla and Nezu, 2007).
3 Communication skills training is a component of DBT (Linehan, 1993) and focuses on ameliorating behavioural processes. Training people in communication skills has been proven to be effective in improving people's lives and reduce their symptoms of mental ill health (Heinssen et al., 2000; Dixon et al., 2001) even with clients with serious and long-standing problems.
4 Behavioural Activation (Linehan, 1993; Hopko et al., 2003; Giesen-Bloo et al., 2006) focuses on the transdiagnostic process of maladaptive behavioural processes.
5 Self-management training (Feldhege, 1979]; van Bilsen and Whitehead, 1994; Cook et al., 2009) has demonstrated its effectiveness in dealing with many behavioural problems and focuses on the transdiagnostic processes of attentional bias and maladaptive behavioural processes.

All these interventions can be found in personality disorder treatment programmes that produced positive results *and* they have been found to be effective in dealing with specific problems. Could the answer for effective treatments for people with personality difficulties lie with Bateman and Fonagy (2000) in combination with the range of evidence-based interventions? This would certainly *not* produce the definitive guidebook of evidence-based protocols for clients with personality problems.

Our suggestion (van Bilsen, 2005) would be to take point four of the list of Bateman and Fonagy as the core issue (theoretical coherence). This demands two things from the therapist. The therapist will need to be able to understand (and convey that understanding to the client) of how the client's problems came into existence and how they are maintained in their current state using a coherent cognitive behavioural theoretical framework. Furthermore the therapist will need to select a range of evidence-based interventions (from the list above) and put them in a chronological order that is in line with the theoretical understanding of clients' problems. There is no need for clinicians to have an all-encompassing theoretical framework that explains all personality problems or disorders. Learning theory and cognitive theories need to be applied to *this* client in order to come to an understanding of *this client's* problems. Based on this understanding the clinician can subsequently compose an idiosyncratic treatment plan based on evidence-based interventions. This would also mean that treatment would really be clear in focus as the treatment would be guided by the individually identified problems of the client and the individually established goals the client has set regarding their problems.

Reflections on Reflections

In this chapter we have reviewed several important issues. Is the term personality disorder a term in a long row of terms that have been used to medicalise and psychologise human phenomena with an aim to control and disenfranchise? We think that this certainly plays a part in the demonising of people with personality disorders but it is not the whole story. There are people with serious and enduring problems, causing harm to themselves and to society. The labelling process of the medical approach may not always be helpful, but it certainly does not cause the problems.

Research into the effectiveness and efficacy of treatments for personality disorders does not present a clear-cut answer in the form of treatment X is far superior to treatment Y. We have some clear guidelines as to which CBT interventions do contribute to treatment outcome and we have guidelines with respect to the organisation of treatment.

It demonstrates to us once more that a categorical approach to personality disorders is a futile quest and that an individualised approach focused on the individualised problem identifications and goal setting is a more productive approach.

Understanding check

Things you should be able to do after reading this chapter:

1 List the personality disorders universally recognised as patterns of maladaptive functioning.
2 Say which CBT interventions have been supported in the treatment of personality disorders.
3 Give four important guidelines for the organisation of personality disorder treatment.

9

PITFALLS FOR THE THERAPIST

The problem

People with a diagnosis of personality disorder are rarely popular with psychological therapists. We have often witnessed groups of clinicians 'duck' when a client with a personality disorder diagnosis needed to be allocated to a therapist. When asked why our colleagues would have such an aversion to working with people who had been diagnosed as 'personality disorder' we would get answers such as:

- Treatment is impossible (therapeutic pessimism).
- They never do what you ask them to do (therapist's shoulds).
- They never tell the truth (therapist over-generalising).
- They are dangerous (over-generalising).
- They will make me feel bad (emotional reasoning by the therapist).
- They are so rigid (therapist's shoulds).

In summary, what our colleagues have told us is that these clients behave exactly as they should behave, as people with personality problems. It may be helpful to refresh our memory regarding the characteristics of people with personality problems: distorted attentional processes (in a rigid and inflexible manner their attention is drawn to issues that are unhelpful); rigid and unhelpful memory processes (whereby they will recall issues that are most self-serving in the maintenance of the problems); reasoning processes are similarly rigid and inflexible and organised towards the maintenance of the problems; maladaptive behaviours to eliminate negative feelings and these behaviours are very habitual.

All these processes have been with the client for a long time and many of these processes result in short-term reinforcement (negative or positive), but longer-term negative consequences. Some examples of this are:

- Self-harm leads to short-term relief of the distress experienced, but results in longer-term feelings of guilt and self-loathing and these once again trigger the distress that leads to the self-harm in the first place.
- Impulsively taking a self-serving opportunity (stealing an unguarded wallet) results in short-term monetary gain but longer-term judicial punishment, which triggers self-serving

cognitions ('I can't help it that people are so careless') and self-pity ('Guess who has the short end of the stick again'), resulting in thoughts of entitlement ('When is it my turn to have a good life?') and the client ruminates about this, which leads to anger and an attentional focus on opportunities to have a good life (for instance by stealing the things he wants).

Many of our colleagues 'blamed' the clients with personality problems for their problems. An example of this is a colleague who would say: 'If they only would behave like my other clients then all would be fine.' This always reminds us of experiences from our past where clinicians demanded clients to stop the problem behaviours before treatment could get offered: problem drinkers needed to stop drinking, fighting couples needed to stop fighting. How would you feel if the car mechanic said to you: 'I will fix your car, but only if you deliver it to the garage in pristine and perfect condition'. So rule number one in working with clients with personality problems is to *expect clients with personality problems*.

Our assumption is that competent CBT is based on applying the elements of the Cognitive Therapy Scale-Revised (CTS-R) (James et al., 2001). Serious deviations from the CTS-R would then be evidence that the therapist has stumbled in a 'pitfall'.

Here are some examples of CTS-R deviations.

Agenda setting

Grant is an experienced cognitive behaviour therapist. In this supervision session he presents that he is getting nowhere with this client. 'It seems that the client just does not want to work in a structured way! Each session is just so chaotic and hectic. The problems seem so overwhelming.' The client is a 27-year-old woman who came to Grant's consulting rooms with a diagnosis of borderline personality disorder. Listening to recordings of Grant's work with this client, we immediately noticed that the client arrives at sessions almost out of breath, and in a rushed, fast-talking way, even before sitting down, starts the session, listing all the things that made her upset in the last week (and many things make her upset) interspersing each complaint with a question ('And what are you going to do about it?') before moving on to the next item on her list. Grant is a kind therapist and he starts his sessions with a polite 'How are you today?' or 'How has your week been?' This is of course very friendly, but it triggers in this client a stream of moments when she has experienced negative feelings. She talks fast, regularly uses words like 'terrible, awful, end of the world for me'. When I ask Grant his reasons for not starting with an agenda, he states that that would have been impolite as the client seems to have so much to talk about. 'She just needs to get it off her chest.' He gives the same reason for not interrupting the client and not guiding her into a more focused discussion.

Absence of conceptual integration

Peter was working with a client who had been given a diagnosis of anti-social personality disorder. Based on the formulation, an important part of the treatment needed to be training this client to adhere more to the generally accepted moral code in society and to learn to experience empathy for the people he was taking advantage of. The sessions were going quite nicely, with good agenda setting, topics such as rational and irrational thinking, working with thought records and problem-solving training were reviewed; but no moral retraining and no empathy training. Peter gave as a reason for not scheduling this as being that he was afraid that it might disrupt the therapeutic relationship with the client. When we reviewed recordings of sessions when Peter had made an attempt to put these topics on the agenda, it was clear that the client's behaviour in these sessions was less co-operative and more sulky; in other words, the client was 'punishing' Peter for doing the right thing.

Forgot about the behaviour, and the feelings and the cognitions

One of our supervisees Sarah was working with a client that had been referred to her with a label of 'has narcissistic personality traits'. This client in his mid-forties would at times burst out in violent rages, triggered by real or imagined slights from other people. Seeking treatment was a condition for not having to go to jail as in the last violent rage he had attacked a colleague. Only the rapid intervention of others prevented this person from being seriously harmed. Sarah brought this client to supervision when she had seen him eight times and she was a bit embarrassed as she had not been able to review any of the anger outburst incidents with the client. This is what happened when we reviewed some recordings. During the agenda setting, all is in perfect order. Sarah announces that this is one of her points for the agenda and the client could not have been more co-operative. However, when the time comes to focus on the events, the client becomes very emotional and states:

> I know I was wrong and have learned so much from it. This has been the best experience of my life, but [now tearful] what about me? My hurt and my pain. It is always other people that get the attention, but I have to do therapy. They can put it behind them, but I am still hurting, I still have to do therapy [now crying and speaking with a loud voice], I should not be sitting here, but they, for what they put me through, for what they made me do [sobbing uncontrollably].

Sarah, being a kind therapist, focuses first on helping the client to calm down and, as a well-trained CBT-therapist, tries to elicit 'hot cognitions' when there are so many negative feelings present. These 'hot cognitions' result in ongoing waves of negative feelings, which sound to Sarah as real distress, and to me as a supervisor, as enormous self-pity.

145

Those readers who were of the opinion that people with personality difficulties are not treatable will by now have perked up and are ready to say: 'See,
they deliberately derail the therapy process; you simply can't work with these
people.' We would politely disagree with this conclusion. This conclusion
assumes that people with personality difficulties deliberately would derail the
therapy process. We don't think so; what these clients demonstrated were the
characteristics of their problems – self-centredness, chaotic thinking, and self-
serving attitude and behaviour. Just as we can't blame the lion for eating the
innocent person who falls into its cage, so we can't blame a person with personality difficulties if these difficulties shine through in the context of therapy.
We have to deploy CBT strategies to counter these problems.

Practising what we preach!

In order to use the correct CBT strategies, we first have to recognise and analyse
the reasons why we are not using them in the first place. In the above-
mentioned examples, the problem was never a lack of knowledge or a lack of
skill in executing the interventions. 'Something' prevented the therapist doing
the right thing. How can we find out what that something is? How would we
do that with a client? If a client is engaging in unhelpful and self-defeating
behaviour and is not able to stop herself or himself, which strategy would any
self-respecting cognitive behaviour therapist aim for? We would try and conduct a functional analysis of the problem, e.g. find out what exactly is the
function of the maladaptive behaviour.

Let's review Grant's interaction with the client who did not wait for agenda
setting but started the session the moment she greeted him in the waiting
room. Table 9.1 shows what we would see if we apply our (SORCC) functional
analysis model. What we have here is the classic CBT set-up of thinking errors,
self-defeating behaviours and negative reinforcement (hypothesised and
feared events do not take place).

Table 9.1

Stimulus	The client arrives at sessions almost out of breath and in a rushed, fast talking way dives into the session, listing all that made her upset in the last week (and many things make her upset), interspersing each complaint with a question (and what are you going to do about it?) before moving on to the next item on her list.
Reaction of therapist (internal)	Thinking: I have got to help her but don't seem to be doing a good job; I should not make life more difficult for her; therapy is for her the only place where she can get these things of her chest, I should not interrupt her, she is just impossible, I can't get a word in.
	Feeling: apprehensive, guilty, irritated, She seems very stressed, I should try to calm her down, talking about agenda setting is so trivial …
	Physiology: sweaty, knot in stomach

(Continued)

Table 9.1 (Continued)

Responses of therapist	Gets very quiet, continues to listen empathically, nodding, hmm-hmming, brief reflections
Consequence	The reaction the therapist dreads most does not happen: client does not get emotionally out of control (negative reinforcement) and does not follow through on her challenge ('what are you going to do about it?'), also negative reinforcement.

So in order to practise what we preach to clients (CBT), we need to be aware and use the same techniques we recommend to clients. Personal signals for the need to practise this self-CBT are:

- Experiencing strong negative feelings in connection with a client's behaviour (feeling very angry when client has not completed homework; feeling very guilty when the client experiences negative feelings; feeling immediately depressed when noticing this client will come in today).
- Experiencing strong positive feelings in connection with the client's behaviour (feeling very happy when the client praises the therapist).
- Deviating consistently from CTS-R-defined good CBT.
- Engaging in excessive self-serving rationalisations to explain CTS-R deviations ('I just had to do it for the client's sake, I (and not my supervisor/manager) know what this client needs').

Practising what we preach means that we take these signals seriously and analyse with a functional analysis what is really happening and use thought records to counter our irrational thinking. This should be followed up with careful monitoring of the therapist's behaviour and emotional experiences during therapy, but also outside therapy.

For clinicians who work frequently with clients with personality problems, we recommend keeping a feeling and worry diary. We would suggest briefly writing down, without any selection, the emotions that each session with a client generates. This is often best done immediately after a session. Furthermore we suggest keeping a worry diary of when the therapist is worrying and/or emoting about a client outside the session. We do not mean to say that any feelings and any worry are pathological – far from it.

When a client you have been working with on stopping his or her self-harm has had a major relapse and is admitted into hospital with some serious self-inflicted injuries; that is disappointing. However, when it leads to the therapist being completely guilt ridden and walking around the clinic crying uncontrollably about what they have put the client through, then it is time for some self-reflection.

By keeping track of the feelings and worries, the therapist can start to become aware of when and how certain clients start to trigger very strong negative/positive feelings that feature prominently in the worries. We would suggest an hour per week of self-reflection in these diaries (Kolb, 1984; Bennett-Levy, 2001, 2006; Bennett-Levy et al., 2001).

Common Pitfalls

- The therapist craves reinforcement from the client. The therapist's emotional balance is in tune with the client's approval or disapproval of therapist behaviour. Therapist experiences strong negative feelings when the client disapproves and excessive positive feelings when the client approves of the therapist. This can often be observed in recordings of therapy sessions, whereby a therapist subtly changes focus when the client expresses negative feelings of any kind. Sometimes the therapist also becomes very protective of the client (I am the only one who really understands this client's predicament).
- The therapist 'should' do this or that. The therapist imposes demands on his/her shoulders: I should help this client, I should be able to solve these problems in four sessions, I should be able to do this (exposure) without the client experiencing any negative feelings; I should never cause my client to feel upset. It is clear that these shoulds are highly irrational and limit the therapeutic room to manoeuvre of the therapist considerably.
- The client 'should' do this or that. The therapist starts 'shoulding' the client. The client should show proper respect, the client should understand, the client should be nice to me ...This kind of should will result in some very strong negative reactions if the client deviates from these shoulds. These reactions can be emotional and behavioural or both. Some therapists become very punitive towards clients when they 'misbehave' in their eyes, while others just feel eaten up with anger and resentment.
- The therapist makes 'private' deals with the client. The therapist has a 'private' understanding with the client. This could be to keep certain issues from the rest of the treatment team, to leave certain items out of the notes or even to do tasks that the client can't do or is not allowed to do.

Reflection on Pitfalls

In this chapter we reviewed a number of pitfalls for therapists in working with personality disorders. At the core of this is of course cognitive and emotional entanglement of the therapist's inner world with that of the client. Being aware of the process and regular self-reflection on one's interactions, emotional and cognitive reactions to clients' behaviours can be helpful in preventing problems. In other words we recommend that therapists practise what they preach and apply CBT to challenging moments with clients.

Understanding check

After reading this chapter you will be able to:

1 Design you own 'pitfall' prevention strategy.
2 Hypothesise about your own personal most likely pitfall.
3 Discuss how the ideas postulated in this chapter could impact on your clinical practice.

REFERENCES

Alden, L.E. and Capreol, M.J. (1993) Avoidant personality disorder: Interpersonal problems as predictors of treatment response. *Behavior Therapy* 24(3): 357–376.

American Psychiatric Association (APA) (2000) *Diagnostic and Statistical Manual of Mental Disorders (DSM-IV-TR).* Arlington, TX: American Psychiatric Publishing.

Annual Review of Clinical Psychology 1: 91–111.

Bandura, A. (1969) *Principles of Behaviour Modification.* New York: Holt, Rinehart & Winston.

Bandura, A. (1986) *Social Foundation of Thought and Action: A Social Cognitive Theory.* Englewood Cliffs, NJ: Prentice Hall.

Bateman, A. and Fonagy, P. (1999) Effectiveness of partial hospitalization in the treatment of borderline personality disorder: A randomized controlled trial. *American Journal of Psychiatry* 156(10): 1563–1569.

Bateman, A.W. and Fonagy, P. (2000) Effectiveness of psychotherapeutic treatment of personality disorder. *British Journal of Psychiatry* 177: 138–143.

Bateman, A.W. and Fonagy, P. (2001) Treatment of borderline personality disorder with psychoanalytically oriented partial hospitalization: An 18-month follow-up. *American Journal of Psychiatry* 158 (1), 36–42.

Bateman, A.W. and Tyrer, P. (2004) Psychological treatment for personality disorders. *Advances in Psychiatric Treatment* 10: 378–388.

Beck, A.T. (1976) *Cognitive Behaviour Therapy and the Emotional Disorders.* New York: International Universities Press.

Beck, A.T., Freeman, A. and Associates (1990) *Cognitive Therapy of Personality Disorders.* New York: Guilford Press.

Beck A.T., Ward, C.H., Mendelson, M., Mock, J. and Erbaugh, J. (1961) An inventory for measuring depression. *Archives of General Psychiatry* 4: 561–71.

Beck, A.T., Rush, A.J., Shaw, B.F. and Emery, G. (1979) *Cognitive Therapy of Depression* (The Guilford Clinical Psychology and Psychopathology Series). New York: Guilford.

Bennett-Levy, James (2001) The value of self-practice of cognitive therapy techniques and self-reflection in the training of cognitive therapists. *Behavioural and Cognitive Psychotherapy* 29: 203–220.

Bennett-Levy, James (2006) Therapist skills: a cognitive model of their acquisition and Refinement, *Behavioural and Cognitive Psychotherapy* 34: 57–78.

Bennett-Levy, J., Turner, F., Beaty, T., Smith, M., Paterson, B. and Farmer, S. (2001) The value of self-practice of cognitive therapy techniques and self-reflection in the training of cognitive therapists. *Behavioural and Cognitive Psychotherapy* 29: 203–220.

Bohus, M., Haaf, B., Stiglmayr, C., Pohl, U., Bohme, R. and Linehan, M. (2000) Evaluation of inpatient dialectical-behavioral therapy for borderline personality disorder – A prospective study. *Behaviour Research & Therapy* 38(9): 875–887.

Brown-Chidsey, R. (2005) *Assessment for Intervention.* New York: Guilford Press.

Brown, G.K., Newman, C.F., Charlesworth, S.E., Crits-Christoph, P. and Beck, A.T. (2004) An open clinical trial of cognitive therapy for borderline personality disorder. *Journal of Personality Disorders* 18: 257–271.

Clarkin, J.F., Foelsch, P.A., Levy, K.N., Hull, J.W., Delaney J.C. and Kernberg, O.F. (2001) The development of a psychodynamic treatment for patients with borderline personality disorder: a preliminary study of behavioral change. *Journal of Personality Disorders* 15, 487–495.

Cold, J., Yang, M., Tyrer, P., Roberts, A. and Ullrich, S. (2006) Prevalence and correlates of personality disorder in Great Britain. *British Journal of Psychiatry* 188: 423–431.

Conrad, P. (1992) Medicalization and social control. *Annual Review of Sociology* 18: 209–232.

Cook, J.A., Copeland, M.E., Hamilton, M.M., Jonikas, J.A., Razzano, L.A., Floyd, C.B., Hudson, W.B., Macfarlane, R.T. and Grey, D.D. (2009) Initial outcomes of a mental illness self-management program based on wellness recovery action planning. *Psychiatric Services* 60: 246–249.

Davidson, K. (2007) *Cognitive Therapy for Personality Disorders*. Abingdon: Routledge.

Davidson, K. and Tyrer, P. (1996) Cognitive therapy for antisocial and borderline personality disorders: Single case series. *British Journal of Clinical Psychology* 35: 413–429.

Denissen, K. and van Bilsen, H.P.J.G. (1987) Motivationele milieu therapie [Motivational milieu therapy]. *Tijdschrift voor Psychotherapie* 13(3): 128–138.

Dixon, L., McFarlane, W.R., Lefley, H., Lucksted, A., Cohen, M., Falloon, I., Mueser, K., Miklowitz, D., Solomon, P. and Sondheimer, D. (2001) Evidence-based practices for services to families of people with psychiatric disabilities. *Psychiatric Services* 52: 903–991.

Dobbert, D. (2007) *Understanding Personality Disorders: An Introduction*. Westport, CT: Greenwood Press.

Domjan, M. (2006) *The Principles of Learning and Behavior: Active Learning Edition*. Belmont, CA: Thomson/Wadsworth.

Duggan, C., Egan, V., Mccarthy, L., Palmer, B. and Lee, A. (2003) Theories of general personality and mental disorder. *British Journal of Psychiatry* 182: 19–23.

D'Zurilla, T.J. and Nezu, A.M. (2007) *Problem Solving Therapy: A Positive Approach to Clinical Intervention*. New York: Springer.

Eells, T.D. (2006) *Handbook of Psychotherapy Case Formulation*. New York: Guilford Press.

Ellis, A. (1970) *The essence of rational psychotherapy: A comprehensive approach to treatment*. New York: Institute for Rational Living.

Elster, Jon (1985) *Sour Grapes: Studies in the Subversion of Rationality*. Cambridge: Cambridge University Press.

Emmelkamp, P.M.G. and Kamphuis, J.H. (2007) *Personality Disorders*. Hove: Psychology Press.

Feldhege, F. (1979) *Selbstkontrolle bei Raushmittelabhangingen klienten*. Munich: Springer.

Festinger, L., Riecken, H. and Schachter, S. (1956) *When Prophecy Fails: A Social and Psychological Study of a Modern Group that Predicted the Destruction of the World*. Minneapolis, MN: University of Minneapolis.

Festinger, L. (1957) *A Theory of Cognitive Dissonance*. Stanford, CA: Stanford University Press.

Foa, E.B. and Rothbaum, B.O. (1998) *Treating the Trauma of Rape: Cognitive Behavior Therapy for PTSD*. New York: Guilford Publications.

Foucault, M. (1988) *Madness and Civilization: A History of Insanity in the Age of Reason*. New York: Vintage.

Gabbett, T. and Hodgson, P. (2003) Incidence of injury in semi-professional rugby league players. *British Journal of Sports Medicine* 37(1): 36–44.

Gambrill, E.D. (1977) *Behavior Modification: Handbook of Assessment, Intervention, and Evaluation*. San Francisco: Jossey-Bass.

Giesen-Bloo, J., van Dyck, R., Spinhoven, P., van Tilburg, W., Dirksen, C., van Asselt, T., Kremers, I., Nadort, M. and Arntz, A. (2006) Outpatient psychotherapy for borderline personality disorder: a randomized trial of schema focused therapy versus transference focused therapy. *Archives of General Psychiatry* 63(6): 649–658.

Goldfried, M. (2003) Cognitive behavior therapy: reflections on the evolution of a therapeutic orientation. *Cognitive Therapy and Research* 27(1): 53–69.

Hare, R.D. (1999) *Without Conscience: The Disturbing World of the Psychopaths among Us.* New York: Guilford Press.

Harvey, A., Watkins, E., Mansell, W. and Shafran, R. (2004) Cognitive behavioural processes across psychological disorders: a transdiagnostic approach to research and treatment. Oxford: Oxford University Press.

Heinssen, R.K., Liberman, R.P. and Kopehwicz, A. (2000) Psychosocial skills training for schizophrenia: lessons from the laboratory. *Schizophrenia Bulletin* 26(1): 21–46.

Hettema, J., Steele, J. and Miller, W.R. (2004) Motivational interviewing, *Annual Review of Clinical Psychology* 1: 91–111.

Hoffman P., A. Fruzzetti, E. Buteau, E.R. Neiditch, D. Penney, M.L. Bruce, F. Hellman and E. Struening. (2005) Family connections: a program for relatives of persons with borderline personality disorder. *Family Process* 44(2): 217–225.

Hopko, D.R., Lejuezb, C.W., Ruggieroc, K.J. and Eifertd, G.H. (2003) Contemporary behavioral activation treatments for depression: Procedures, principles, and progress. *Clinical Psychology Review* 23: 699–717.

Huband, N., McMurran, M., Evans, C. and Duggan, C. (2007) Social problem- solving plus psychoeducation for adults with personality disorder: Pragmatic randomised controlled trial. *British Journal of Psychiatry* 190: 307–313.

James, I.A., Blackburn, I-M., Reichelt, F.K., Garland, A. and Armstrong, P. (2001) *Manual of the Revised Cognitive Therapy Scale (CTS-R).* Northumberland: Tyne and Wear NHS Trust.

Kendall, P.C. and Brasswell, L.B. (1985) *Cognitive Behavioural Modification with Impulsive Children.* New York: Guilford.

Kingdon, D.G. and Turkington, D. (1991) The use of cognitive behaviour therapy with a normalising rationale in schizophrenia. *Journal of Nervous and Mental Disease* 179, 207–211.

Kolb, D. (1984) *Experiential Learning: Experience as the Source of Learning and Development.* Englewood Cliffs, NJ: Prentice Hall.

Landelijke Stuurgroep Multidisciplinaire Richtlijnontwikkeling in de GGZ (2008) *Multidisciplinaire Richtlijn Persoonlijkheidsstoornissen. Richtlijn voor de diagnostiek en behandeling van volwassen patiënten met een persoonlijkheidsstoornis.* Utrecht: Uitgever: Trimbos-instituut (art. no.: AF0806).

Lazarus, A.A. (1981) *The Practice of Multimodal Therapy.* New York: McGraw-Hill.

Leichsenring, F. and Leibing, E. (2003) The effectiveness of psychodynamic therapy and cognitive behavior therapy in the treatment of personality disorders: a meta-analysis. *American Journal of Psychiatry* 160: 1223–1232.

Lenzenweger, M.F., Lane, M.C., Loranger, A.W. and Kessler, R.C. (2007) DSM-IV personality disorders in the National Comorbidity Survey Replication. *Biological Psychiatry* 62(6): 553–564.

Lewin, K. (1935) *A Dynamic Theory of Personality.* New York: McGraw-Hill.

Lewin, K. (1936) *Principles of Topological Psychology.* New York: McGraw-Hill.

Lewin, K. (1948) *Resolving Social Conflicts; Selected Papers on Group Dynamics,* ed. Gertrude W. Lewin. New York: Harper & Row.

Linehan, M.M. (1993) *Cognitive-Behavioural Treatment of Borderline Personality Disorder.* New York: Guilford Press.

Linehan, M.M., Heard, H. and Armstrong, H.E. (1993) Naturalistic follow-up of a behavioural treatment for chronically parasuicidal borderline patients. *Archives of General Psychiatry* 50: 971–977.

151

Linehan, M.M., Schmidt, H., Dimeff, L.A., Craft, J.C. and Comtois, K.K.A. (1999) Dialectical behavior therapy for patients with borderline personality disorder and drug-dependence. *American Journal on Addictions* 8(4): 279–292.

Linehan, M.M., Tutek, D.A. and Armstrong, H.E. (1994) Interpersonal outcome of cognitive behavioral treatment for chronically suicidal borderline patients. *American Journal of Psychiatry* 151(12): 1771–1776.

Livesley, J. (2003) *Practical Management of Personality Disorders*. New York: Guilford.

Mahoney, M.J. (1977) Reflections on the cognitive learning trend in psychotherapy. *American Psychologist* 32: 5–13.

Mash, E.J. and Barkley, R.A. (2007) *Assessment of Childhood Disorders*. New York: Guilford Press.

McQuillan, A., Nicastro, R., Guenot, F., Girard, M., Lissner, C. and Ferrero, F. (2005) Intensive dialectical behavior therapy for outpatients with borderline personality disorder who are in crisis. *Psychiatric Services* 56: 193–197.

Meares, R., Stevenson, J. and Comerford, A. (1999) Psychotherapy with borderline patients: I. A comparison between treated and untreated cohorts. *Australian and New Zealand Journal of Psychiatry* 33: 467–472.

Miller, W.R. and Rollnick, S. (2002) *Motivational Interviewing: Preparing People for Change*. New York: Guilford.

Millon, T. et al. (1998) *Psychopathy: Antisocial, Criminal and Violent Behavior*. Guilford Press.

Morey, L.C. (1997) *The Personality Assessment Screener Professional Manual*. Lutz, FL: Psychological Assessment Resources.

National Institute for Health and Clinical Excellence (2005) *Personality Disorder – Everybody's Business*. London: NICE.

Nezu, A.M., and Lombardo, E. (2004) *Cognitive-behavioral Case Formulation to Treatment Design*. New York: Springer.

Nordahl, H.M. and Nysaeter, T.E. (2005) Schema therapy for patients with borderline personality disorder: a single case series. *Journal of Behavior Therapy and Experimental Psychiatry* 36: 254–264.

Oei, Tian P.S. and Baranoff, J. (2007) Young Schema Questionnaire: Review of psychometric and measurement issues. *Australian Journal of Psychology*, 59(2): 78–86.

Padesky, C. (1990) *Principles and Methods: Cognitive Therapy for Personality Disorders*. Audio CD. Huntington Beach, CA: Centre for Cognitive Therapy.

Palmer, S. (1992) Multimodal assessment and therapy: A systematic, technically eclectic approach to counselling, psychotherapy and stress management. *Counselling* 3(4): 220–224.

Palmer, S. and Dryden, W. (1991) A multimodal approach to stress management. *Stress News, Journal of the International Stress Management Association* 3(1): 2–10.

Palmer, S. and Dryden, W. (1995) *Counselling for Stress Problems*. London: Sage.

Palmer, S., Davidson, K., Tyrer, P., Gumley, A., Tata, P., Norrie, J., Murray, H. and Seivewright, H. (2006) The cost-effectiveness of cognitive behavior therapy for borderline personality disorder: results from the Boscot trial, *Journal of Personality Disorders* 20(5): 466–481.

Paris, J. (2005) Recent advances in the treatment of borderline personality disorder. *Canadian Journal of Psychiatry* 50(8): 1579–1583.

Parker, G. and Hadzi-Pavlovic, D. (2001) *A Question of Style: Refining the Dimensions of Personality Disorder Style* 15(4): 300–318.

Perry, J.C., Banon, E. and Ianni, F. (1999) Effectiveness of psychotherapy for personality disorders. *American Journal of Psychiatry* 156: 1312–1321.

Piper, W.E., McCallum, M., Joyce, A.S., Azim, H.F. and Ogrodniczuk, J.S. (1998) Interpretive and supportive forms of psychotherapy and patient personality variables. *Journal of Consulting and Clinical Psychology* 66: 558–567.

Piper, W.E., McCallum, M., Joyce, A.S. and Azim, H.F. (1999) Follow-up findings for interpretive and supportive forms of psychotherapy and patient personality variables. *Journal of Consulting and Clinical Psychology* 67: 267–273.

Premack, D. (1959) Towards empirical behavior laws: positive reinforcement, *Psychological Review* 66: 219–233.

Prochaska, J.O., DiClemente, C.C. and Norcross, J.C. (1992) In search of how people change: Applications to addictive behaviors. *American Psychologist* 47(9): 1102–1114.

Rendu, A., Moran, P., Patel, A., Knapp, M. and Mann, A. (2002) Economic impact of personality disorders in UK primary care attenders. *British Journal of Psychiatry* 181: 62–66.

Roth, A. and Fonagy, P. (2004) *What Works for Whom?* New York: Guilford.

Ryle, A. and Golynkina, K. (2000) Effectiveness of time-limited cognitive analytic therapy of borderline personality disorder: factors associated with outcome. *British Journal of Medical Psychology* 73: 197–210.

Smith, K., Shah, A. and Wright, K. (1995) The prevalence and costs of psychiatric disorders and learning disabilities. *British Journal of Psychiatry* 166: 9–18.

Stevenson, J. and Meares, R. (1992) An outcome study of psychotherapy for patients with borderline personality disorder. *American Journal of Psychiatry* 149: 358–362.

Sturmey, P. (2007) *Functional Analysis in Clinical Treatment*. New York: Academic Press.

Svartberg, M., Stiles, T.C. and Seltzer, M.H. (2004) Randomized, controlled trial of the effectiveness of short-term dynamic psychotherapy and cognitive therapy for cluster C personality disorders. *American Journal of Psychiatry* 161: 810–817.

Tyrer, P., Sensky, T. and Mitchard, S. (2003) The principles of nidotherapy in the treatment of persistent mental and personality disorders. *Psychotherapy and Psychosomatics* 72: 350–356.

van Bilsen, H.P.J.G. (1984) Heroïne gebruiken: Een (literatuur) studie naar de gebruiksmogelijkheden [Using heroin: A (literature) study of the possibilities]. *Tijdschrift voor Alcohol, Drugs en Andere Psychotrope Stoffen* 10(4): 154–157.

van Bilsen, H.P.J.G. (1985a) Praktische problemen in de ambulante gedragstherapie bij heroïneverslaafden [Practical problems in the ambulatory behavior therapy among heroin addicts]. *Gedragstherapie* 18(1): 77–86.

van Bilsen, H.P.J.G. (1985b) Valkuilen voor de therapeut: verslavingsproblemen [Pitfalls for the therapist: Addiction problems]. *Tijdschrift voor Psychotherapie* 11(3): 192–195.

van Bilsen, H.P.J.G. (1986a) Heroin addiction: Morals revisited. *Journal of Substance Abuse Treatment* 3(4): 279–284.

van Bilsen, H.P.J.G. (1986b) Moraliseren of normaliseren: Een psychologische visie op de hulpverlening aan zogenaamd ongemotiveerde heroïneverslaafden in methadonprogramma's [Moralization or normalization: A psychological view of the treatment of so-called unmotivated heroin addicts in methadone programs]. *Tijdschrift voor Alcohol, Drugs en Andere Psychotrope Stoffen* 12(5): 182–189.

van Bilsen, H.P.J.G. (1991) Motivational interviewing: Perspectives from the Netherlands, with particular emphasis on heroin dependent clients. In W.R. Miller and S. Rollnick (eds) *Motivational Interviewing: Preparing People to Change Addictive Behaviour*. New York: Guilford.

van Bilsen, H.P.J.G. (1992) Verslaving, een fenomeen met veel gezichten [Addiction: A phenomenon with many faces]. *Tijdschrift voor Alcohol, Drugs en Andere Psychotrope Stoffen* 18(2): 70–80.

van Bilsen, H.P.J.G. (1995a) Motivation as a precondition and bridge between unmotivated client and overmotivated therapist. In H.P.J.G. van Bilsen, C. Kendall-Philip and Jan Slavenburg (eds) *Behavioral Approaches for Children and Adolescents: Challenges for the Next Century*. New York: Plenum Press.

van Bilsen, H.P.J.G. (1995b) Unused opportunities for behaviour therapy in education. In H.P.J.G. van Bilsen, C. Kendall-Philip and Jan Slavenburg (eds) *Behavioral Approaches for Children and Adolescents: Challenges for the Next Century*. New York: Plenum Press.

van Bilsen, H.P.J.G. (2005) Making treatment for personality disorders effective: back to basics. *BABCP Magazine-Research Digest* 33.

van Bilsen, H.P.J.G. and van Emst, A.J. (1986) Heroin addiction and motivational milieu therapy. *International Journal of the Addictions* 21(6): 707–713.

van Bilsen, H.P.J.G. and van Emst, A.J. (1989) Motivating drug users. In G. Bennett (ed.) *Treating Drug Abusers*. London: Routledge.

van Bilsen, H.P.J.G. and Whitehead, B. (1994) Learning controlled drugs use: A case study. *Behavioural & Cognitive Psychotherapy* 22(1): 87–95.

van Bilsen, H.P.J.G. and Wilke, M. (1998) Drug and alcohol abuse in young people In Philip Jeremy Graham (ed.) *Cognitive-behaviour Therapy for Children and Families*, New York: Cambridge University Press.

van Bilsen, H.P.J.G., Engelen, T. and Volker, S. (1993) *Gedragstherapie in de klas* [Behaviour therapy in the Classroom]. Rotterdam: Swets & Zeitlinger.

van Bilsen, H.P.J.G., Kendall, P.C. and Slavenburg, J.H. (eds) (1995) *Behavioral Approaches for Children and Adolescents: Challenges for the Next Century*. New York: Plenum Press.

van Bilsen, H.P.J.G., Jonkers, J., Schuurman, C.M. and Swager, H.D. (1991) Geïntegreerde behandeling van sociale-vaardigheidstekorten bij kinderen uit het speciaal onderwijs [Integrated treatment of social skill deficits in children from special education]. *Kind en Adolescent* 12(2): 78–86.

Van Emst, A.J. and van Bilsen, H.P.J.G. (1989) Alcoholproblemen onder ouderen [Alcohol problems among the elderly]. *Tijdschrift voor Alcohol, Drugs en Andere Psychotrope Stoffen* 15(3): 87–97.

Verheul, R. (2005) Clinical utility of dimensional models for personality pathology. *Journal of Personality Disorders* 19: 283–302.

Verheul, R., van den Bosch, L.M., Koeter, M.W., de Ridder, M.A.J., Stijnen, T. and van den Brink, W. (2003) Dialectical behaviour therapy for women with borderline personality disorder: 12-month, randomised clinical trial in The Netherlands. *British Journal of Psychiatry* 182: 135–140.

Warren, F., Preedy-Fayers, K., McGauley, G., Pickering, A., Norton, K., Geddes, J.R. and Dolan, B. (2003) *Review of Treatments for Severe Personality Disorder*. Home Office Report. London: Home Office.

Watson, D. and Tharp, R. (2006) *Self Directed Behavior*. Chichester: Wiley.

Widiger, T.A. (1992) Categorical versus dimensional classification: Implications from and for research. *Journal of Personality Disorders* 6: 287–300.

Winston, A., Laikin, M., Pollack, J., Samstag, L.W., McCullough, L. and Muran, J.C. (1994) Short-term psychotherapy of personality disorders. *American Journal of Psychiatry* 151: 190–194.

Winston, A., Pollack, J., McCullough, L., Flegenheimer, W., Kestenbaum, R. and Trujillo, M. (1991) Brief psychotherapy of personality disorders. *Journal of Nervous and Mental Disease* 179: 188–193.

Wolpe, J. (1958) *Psychotherapy by Reciprocal Inhibition*. Stanford, CA: Stanford University Press.

Wolpe, J. (1964) *The Conditioning Therapies: The Challenge in Psychotherapy*. New York: Holt, Rinehart and Winston.

Wolpe, J. and Lazarus, A. (1966) *Behavior Therapy Techniques: A Guide to the Treatment of Neuroses*. Oxford: Pergamon Press.

Young, J.E., Klosko, J.S. and Weishaar, M.E. (2003) *Schema Therapy: A Practitioner's Guide*. New York: Guilford Press.

INDEX

Tables and Figures are indicated by page numbers in **bold**.

collaboration, 126
  in agenda setting, 20, 21, 23, 85
  lack of, 90–1
'Colombo technique', 131
communication skills, 111, 140
compassionate-based CBT, 17
conditioning, 30–2
conflict reflections, 129
Conrad, P., 135
consequences of problem behaviour, 48, 50
  expected and actual, 54
contemplation (stage in change), 120
  and precontemplation, 119
contingencies, 48–9, 50
Cook, J.A. et al., 140
core beliefs, **35**, 68, 108–9
cost of personality disorders, 136, 139
counter-therapeutic behaviours, 87–94
  between sessions, 90–2
  during sessions, 89
cure and care, 136

Davidson, K., 99
Davidson, K. and Tyrer, P., 140
demanding thinking, 12
demands on clients, 126
Denissen, K. and van Bilsen, H.P.J.G., 123
dependent personality disorder (DPD), 8
depression, 6, 30, 40, 43, 45, 67–8
determination/decision to change,
    120–1, 122
  and self-efficacy, 127–8
'devil's advocate' technique, 131
Diagnostic and Statistical Manual of Mental
    Disorders, 3, 4
dialectical behaviour therapy (DBT), 17, 137,
    138, 140
dimensional and dichotomous model,
    10, 15
discrepancy between present reality and
    goals, 126–7
disqualifying the positive, 38
Dixon, L et al., 140
Dobbert, D., 3, 4, 7, 8
Domjan, M., 18
drugs and alcohol, 58, 60, 135
DTRs (daily thought records), 98–108
  behaviour in, 106, **107–8**
  example, **103–6**
  externalising of dialogues, 100
  instructions, **101–3**
  learning to do, 99
  recognising rational thinking, 99
  repetition, 99
  'yesterday-ing', 100–1
Duggan, C. et al., 10

Dutch Institute for the Development of
    Clinical Guidelines (Trimbos Instituut),
    136–7
D'Zurilla and Nezu, 113, 140

education in CBT interventions, 27–9, 126
Eells, T.D., 47, 88
eliciting factors of problem behaviour, 53
Ellis, A., 17
emotional/cognitive reasoning, 39
empathy with client, 127
ending therapy, 75–7, **76**
evaluation of sessions, 81, **82**
evaluation of treatment, 73–5, **74**
evidence base for treatment of personality
    disorders, 136–9
  for CBT, 135, 137, 138
  criteria for effectiveness (Bateman and
      Tyrer), 137–8
  severe disorders, 138
  treatment guidelines (Bateman and
      Fonagy), 138–9
evidence-based guidelines, 98
evocation of issues, 126
expectations of behaviours, 53–4
expressing positive and negative feelings,
    110, 112
externalising of dialogues, 100

feedback from clients, 61–3, 78, 81, **82**
feeling diary, 147
feeling reflections, 129
feelings
  and behaviour, 70–1
  and brain, 68–9
  and cognitions, 57
  expressing (positive and negative),
      110, 112
  healthy and unhealthy, 39–40
  intensity of, 39–40
  and life events, 67
Feldhege, F., 97, 140
Festinger, L., 122
Festinger, L. et al., 122
fine-tuned reflections, 129–**30**
Foa, E.B. and Rothbaum, B.O., 13
formulation, 55–63, **61**, **62–3**, 79, 88
  BASIC-ID (Behaviour Affect Sensations
      Interpersonal Cognitive Imagery
      Drugs and Alcohol), 50, 55–8, 59–61
  necessity for, 94
Foucault, M., 135
functional analysis (FA), 53–5

Gabbett, T. and Hodgson, P., 139
Gambrill, E.D., 72

thinking
  and behaviour, 17, 39
  and feelings, 57
  irrational, 36, 38–9, 67, 71
  recognising rational thinking, 99
  see also DTRs (daily thought records)
thought processes, 12, 14
topographical analysis (TA), 51–**2**
  see also functional analysis (FA)
transdiagnostic processes, 10–15
transference-focused psychotherapy, 137
treatment
  based on individual formulations, 140–1
  and cost, 139
  multi-faceted, 140
  value of, 139
trust in process of change, 122
types of personality disorders, 4–8, 10

UK
  cost of personality disorders, 136
  prevalence of personality disorder, 136
USA
  drugs and alcohol use, 135

USA *cont.*
  prevalence of personality disorder, 135–6
usefulness of beliefs, 109

values of therapists, 87
van Bilsen, H.P.J.G., 123, 125, 135, 141
van Bilsen, H.P.J.G. and van Emst, A.J., 123
van Bilsen, H.P.J.G. and Whitehead, B., 140
van Bilsen, H.P.J.G. and Wilke, M., 123
Verheul, R., 10, 140
Verheul, R. et al., 138

Warren, F. et al., 138
Watson, D. and Tharp, R., 95
Widiger, T.A., 10
Winston, A. et al., 137
Wolpe, J., 10
Wolpe, J. and Lazarus, A., 10
work between sessions, 81
working with difficult clients, 87–8, 143–4
written agreements on tasks, 92

'yesterday-ing', 100–1
Young, J.E. et al., 138, 140

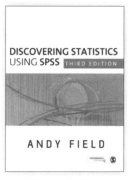
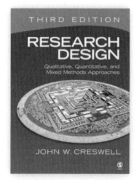

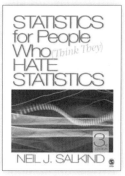

Research Methods Books from SAGE

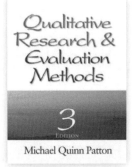

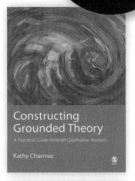

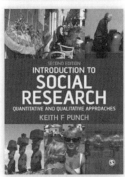

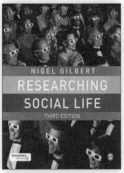

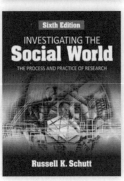

www.sagepub.co.uk